The Secret Green Sauce

Best Practices for Growing *Green* Revenues

By Bill Roth
Green Business Coach
Entrepreneur.com

Bill Roth

Copyright 2009
Printed in the United States
First Edition 2009

ISBN: 978-0-9819945-3-6

Acknowledgements:

Much thanks to the profiled business leaders and entrepreneurs for their contribution of time and knowledge.

Fred Fassett is my publisher. He did a yeoman's job of herding the cats to move my manuscript into publication.

Thomas Morris did an outstanding job designing the book's engaging cover.

This book is dedicated to my daughter Taylor and son Clayton. I hope my documentation of how to make money going green will create a safer and cleaner world for you to live in.

Table of Content

"The Secret Green Sauce"

"The Secret *Green* Sauce™"

As the Green Business Coach for Entrepreneur.com I am continuously being contacted by business people from across the country trying to figure out what "going green" could mean for their business.

These are the three questions I get asked most often:

- *"Can you* make money going green?"
- *"How do* you make money going green?"
- *"How do* you grow *green* revenues?"

This book answers these questions by profiling ***the best practices* being used by pioneering businesses and entrepreneurs that are making money by going green.**

I assembled these best practices through a two-year effort of searching for, and interviewing, the business pioneers who are successfully building green businesses and launching green products.

*This book reveals their
"secret green sauce" for making money!*

Can You Make Money Going Green?

Yes. This chapter outlines why the world will be adopting the principals of sustainability. But the *hot news* is that financial documentation is now emerging that more sustainable companies have higher stock valuations than their less sustainable competitors. *JUMP to Chapter Seven if you are an investor or CFO looking to out perform the market by 400 basis points!!*

7

The Green Economic Revolution is what I labeled this global adoption of sustainability in my introductory April 2008 Entrepreneur.com column. It is a revolution because the systems used during the 20th Century to operate the world are either being radically re-engineered or replaced.

The Economics

The three mega-trends propelling this Green Economic Revolution are:

1. The Collapse of "Unsustainability"
    20th Century's business systems are increasingly *costing more and delivering less*. They are becoming unsustainable in terms of their economics and environmental/societal costs. **The competitive decline of these systems are opening the door to businesses offering solutions that *"cost less, mean more"*.**

2. The Emergence Of The Awareness Customer™
    Three hugely powerful groups of consumers are now buying sustainability based upon their increasing awareness that change must occur to fulfill their self-interest. The purchasing power of these three groups exceeds that of the combined Gross National Products of China, Japan, United Kingdom and France.

3. Economies of Scale
    Price competitiveness is the key to the global adoption of sustainability. And sustainability's products and services are just now achieving the economics of scale that allow them to compete on price with the 20th Century's solutions that are in an upward price spiral.

Combined, these three mega-trends of the Green Economic Revolution are propelling the world toward a tipping point in time where "going green" achieves price competitiveness compared to the 20th Century's unsustainable solutions.

$10 Trillion Annual Global Green Economy

As a professional economist I built a financial model attempting to project the Green Economic Revolution's global business market size. The first model I did was in early 2008. At that time I went way out on a limb compared to consensus assessments and projected a $1 trillion global market in ten years for sustainable goods and services.

I have now revised this model based upon these two assumptions:

1. The prices for legacy 20th Century goods and services face an upward price curve *as global demand* for everything from water to oil to food to scarce metals, etc. exceeds the 20th Century systems' supply capabilities. For example, finding more oil is not reducing the price at the pump. Regional shortages in water supply cannot be solved by creating more "free" clean water. Global food supplies are not meeting global demand and their unintended health consequences are increasing health care costs.

2. Sustainable goods and services are now entering production economies-of-scale that are driving down their prices while delivering solutions to the world's environmental, energy-supply and wellness challenges.

Earth 2017 ***Pricing*** Tipping Point

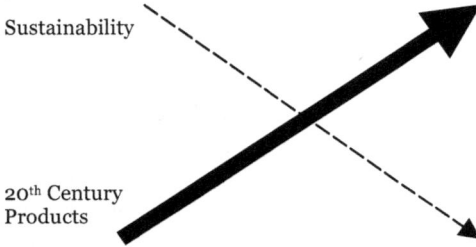

Sustainability

20th Century
Products

My analysis now projects the following two very stunning results:

1. ***As early as 2017***, the price tipping point will have occurred where going green no longer means paying more.

2. At the anticipated point-in-time when sustainability is price competitive with 20th Century solutions **the annual global market size for sustainability solutions will be $10 trillion!**

But the key point of this book is
that the opportunity is now!

The businesses and entrepreneurs I profile in this book have already achieved being price competitive and green. By doing so they are experiencing exceptional revenue growth and they are winning market share against competitors attempting to protect/preserve legacy 20th Century products.

How Do You Make Money Going Green?

The Secret Green Sauce™ question that successful green-entrepreneurs/businesses are answering is:

> *"How can I make my green-business
> the least cost solution?"*

Their answer is offering customers LOWER COSTS, MORE MEANING.

Here are some of the companies profiled in this book that are on this path:

Give Something Back is the largest independent office supply company in Northern California. They are expanding their sales state-wide and into other states. Much of their revenues come from blind bids selected by the purchasing entity based upon price. Yet, they average selling 60-80% recycled paper compared to the industry average of 10%!

Amanda's is a healthy fast food restaurant that is competitive on price, convenience and taste. Amanda's sells natural meat cheeseburgers and organic foods served with 100% re-compostable napkins and utensils. In this recession where restaurant closures are up compared to 2008 including three within walking distance of Amanda's location, this store is achieving year-over-year sales increase results.

The Ritz Carlton on Maui has a marketing program featuring Jean-Michel Cousteau's Ambassadors of the Environment to attract customers and to enrich the experience of their guests by offering educational opportunities tied to learning about the environment. It started as a program for their guest's children. Then the parents, hearing how much fun their kids were having, began to ask if they could participate also. As part of expanding this program *they now have an on-site organic garden growing native food that is served in their restaurant that is <u>increasing the hotel's food revenues</u>*.

My local Ace Hardware store is confronting intense competition from a big box retailer that moved into our small suburban town a couple of years ago. This Ace Hardware store is differentiating themselves from their big box competition by engaging customers on what to buy to enhance their home's air indoor quality, to reduce their children's exposure to pesticides by buying organic products and by reducing their electric bills with energy efficiency lights.

First Solar has a vision for roof top solar systems that are price competitive with utility supplied electricity. They project this can be achieved at a $1 per watt manufacturing costs. When I first met them in 2004 their panel manufacturing costs were around $2.50 per watt and they were building their business with early adopter customers in Europe and California. They now represent their manufacturing costs as below $1 per watt, they have a manufacturing capacity about equal in size to a nuclear power plant and their stock is selling for around 8 times their initial public offering stock price! And they just announced a massive 2,000 MW project in China.

Rainforest Alliance certifies coffees based upon the criteria of "tastes great, good for farmers and best for earth." Rainforest Alliance Certified coffee are grown on farms where forests are protected, where rivers, soils and wildlife are conserved and workers are treated with respect including being paid decent wages, being properly equipped and having access to education and medical care. *Their certified coffees are averaging approximately 100% annual sales growth (meaning sales double each year compared to the prior year!).* Companies that sell their certified coffee include Walmart. Whole Foods, Caribou Coffee and Mars Drinks. They can be found in 50,000 supermarkets, convenience stores, cafes, restaurants and corporate offices worldwide.

Habitat Suites in Austin, Texas has the business motto of "Environmental consciousness in action." They provide a hotel environment free of toxic chemicals including pesticides, they have built the largest solar system on a hotel in the continental U.S. and they have developed their property's four acres as a garden growing organic fruits and vegetables served to guests, given to work associates and contributed to local food-banks. What has impressed me is their repeat-customer business. A major contributor to this high repeat customer business is how well the guests sleep. Their quests continuously check out with comments on what a great night's sleep they experienced. And the hotel's staff believes their guests are sleeping so well because the hotel is free of toxic chemical. Habitat Suites is price competitive but they have a great repeat business because their competition can't compete on their ability to offer a great night's rest!

Frog Hollow Farm founded by Al Courchesne is a classic case study on how to push all the right buttons in building a green business. Al organically grows fruit so delicious they are listed by brand name on the menu at Chez Panisse, Alice Water's fountain-head restaurant of organic and locally produced foods. Al used brand leveraging with Whole Foods to grow his brand equity and has developed a multi-channel sales strategy that produces year round revenues and

13

attractive margins. He even gave me the term Terroir that I use as the title of Chapter Nine on The Secret Green Sauce™ of green entrepreneurship.

Apple is so cool they don't even promote how their pioneering designs are a leading example of how to grow green revenues. They have sold 6 billion iTunes at 99 cents a song via digital downloads which *epitomize the grow-green-revenue mantra of "less cost, more meaning"* (Chapter Two, The Awareness Customer™).

Canyon Construction and *Diefenbach Development* are two companies that are surviving this home construction crash as green contractors. Canyon Construction built a platinum LEED certified corporate headquarters building to demonstrate the commercial and technical viability of going green to their growing list of customers looking to live in homes that are sustainable in terms of their family's health and carbon footprint. Diefenbach Development licenses cutting edge technologies and uses them as a marketing tool to win bids from early-adopter customers by offering innovative construction solutions that are price competitive and sustainable.

Clorox has developed the ability to look "inside the minds" of Concerned Caregivers, one of the key groups driving the adoption of buying green. Their Green Works product (sold at Walmart and other big box retailers) is the poster child for how to build a green marketing plan to achieve market-share leading, significantly sized, annual revenues.

Walmart may be remembered by history as the company that did the most to introduce sustainability as a path for growing revenues and profits. They are involved in a massive, global, re-engineering around sustainability that is impacting how they operate, who they buy from and what they sell. *They are implementing "Sustainability 2.0"* (Chapter Five, "Know It, Embrace It").

Palm Desert, California is obviously not a company. But I include this city as a case study because The Secret Green Sauce™ of green-entrepreneurship is growing in communities across America supported by mayors and city council-members. Palm Desert has pioneered a loan process where homeowners and businesses can borrow money from the city to invest in higher efficiency air conditioners and solar panels. The homeowner or business pays the loan back through their property taxes. This program has a goal for pumping $45 million of new business activity into the community creating entrepreneurs like Renova Energy Corporation that I profile in Chapter Three-Pricing. Palm Desert's green-entrepreneurial spirit is creating lower electric bills for their citizens, lower emissions by their host utility and green jobs/entrepreneurs that support their community's economic development. And by the way, their elected officials are all Republicans. As City Councilman Jim Ferguson (R) explains, "This is not a partisan issue. It is a common sense issue."

How To Grow Green Revenues

Here's the best practices recipe ingredients of *The Secret Green Sauce*™ for growing green revenues being used by companies like those listed above:

1. Align value with values

2. Prove It, Conclusively!

3. "Know it, Embrace it."

This list might look so obvious or simple you will be tempted to not read on. Please don't make that mistake. If it were truly this obvious everyone would be doing it.

For example, everyone knows that achieving price leadership can increase revenues, including green revenues. But I really don't know of any green products that begin as price leaders. The winners profiled in this book have deployed a "Crossing the Green-Pricing Chasm™" strategy which wins sales with early-adopter customers that then enables a path for building to price leadership.

The first step in Crossing the Pricing Chasm™
*is to "**align value with values**,"*
vs. "align values with value."

Values are where so many green businesses and entrepreneurs begin. <u>In my world of economics the winners are the ones who offer the best value</u> defined by the consumer's product expectations on price and quality. "Doing right" is socially and environmentally valuable but if the customer is not willing to pay for it then you have the recipe for business failure. As Marianne Wu, Partner at Mohr Davidow, one of Silicon Valley's leading venture capital firms explained at the Always On Going Green Conference in September 2009:

16

"Green doesn't sell just because it is green
but also because the economics work."

I actually profile my wife's home remodeling consultancy business to provide an example of how aligning value and values is the path for winning customers and selling more. And I provide documentation on how this is also a path for achieving superior stock valuation in Chapter Seven, "Increase Stockholder Value!"

The business of selling sustainability is now in the throes of what economists call an "emerging market." Customers are trying to figure out if sustainability is something they want to buy, who to believe in the evaluation of a product and ultimately who to buy from. At this moment there is great consumer confusion. A lot of companies and industries are spending big bucks advertising they are green. But consumer reaction is often disbelief and distrust of the advertising. Consumers are very uncertain, bordering upon jaundiced distrust, over the competing green business claims being made. And even worse, too much of business advertising is "green-washing" where companies are "spinning" a green image that is not supported by all of the facts. At the other extreme are websites that are "Dark Green" and merchants I call "techno-green" that overwhelm consumers with details, analysis and often, preaching.

In this confusing emerging market the green business winners are bending over backwards attempting to prove themselves and their products. I call this "Prove it, Conclusively." Candidly, I have never seen such an effort. And it will only be increasing in scale as the government introduces new regulations and definitions emerge for products and business activities that we have never really measured before like a "carbon footprint."

Even if your business products are price competitive on something that the consumer values but you miss this step of "Prove It, Conclusively!" then you will be relegated in market size to being just a niche player. Unfortunately I know of many good companies with great green products now in this situation. Chapter Four, "Prove It, Conclusively!" outlines the best practices of successful green companies for gaining the consumer's confidence and business.

Finally, "Know it, Embrace it" is a what a leader in Web 2.0 communications shared with me as the key to understanding how it works, and how it can work for selling green. If you are still one of the few who are not on Face Book or Twitter then for definitional purposes I define Web 2.0 as a communal world of internet-interactive-sharing of information and education.

The growth of Web 2.0 directly ties to the consumer's jaundiced concerns regarding green-washing. It is a dynamic I capture graphically in Chapter Five that shows how customers are using Web 2.0 to achieve Sustainability 2.0. The process is one where early adopter consumers of sustainable goods and services figure out what to buy and from whom and then through tweets and blogs they contribute this learning toward a collective consensus.

I give a lot of speeches that appear to impress my audience based upon the insights I provide on sustainability and its pace of adoption. One audience question I am typically asked is:

"How did you learn about this?"

My answer is Web 2.0. It is a rich resource being mined by companies seeking green customers.

But Web 2.0 is not something you penetrate or influence as Corporate America is finding out. This is a self-governing learning system of brutal honesty that instructs, educates and informs. And those that know, embrace, because the facts are so compelling and the source is so legitimate. If you want to grow green revenues then "Know it, Embrace it" and by doing so you will not only be aligning with your key customers but also gaining competitive advantage against legacy companies that still are mired in "Tell them, sell them" or who think "Know it, Embrace it" means sending out tweet surveys that are motion, not facilitation.

Green Will Stimulate Your Sales!

As I write this book the world is in a recession. Businesses need to sell and consumers need a reason to buy. *The opportunity of the Green Economic Revolution for business is that it creates a compelling reason for a consumer to buy.*

For example, we need to massively replace our current fleet of low-mileage gasoline cars with alternatives that reduce emissions and our dependence upon foreign oil. There are an estimated 250 million automobiles in the United States. Converting them during the next ten years to automobiles that can travel at least the 35.5 miles to the gallon mileage-standard for new cars recently established by the Obama administration (lower than what a Prius can achieve) will generate approximately $650 billion in annual "green revenues."

We need a food system that produces healthy and tasty food that is price competitive and will contribute toward lowering health care costs by improving our nutrition. Hoovers estimates there are approximately

200,000 "fast food restaurants" with $120 billion in annual revenues. Shifting 50% of this annual revenue into organic, locally produced food of high nutritional value would generate $50 billion a year in "green revenues," lower health care costs and reduce the carbon footprint of a food-transportation system that requires approximately 1500 miles to deliver the food you eat.

We need to re-engineer our homes and offices to save money on water and energy. In so doing we will improve indoor air quality which will also contribute toward reducing health care costs. There are approximately 100 million houses in the United States (not counting apartments). If every homeowner spent $10,000 upgrading their home's ceiling insulation, caulking their windows, installing low flow toilets and installing instantaneous water heaters then this effort would generate $1 trillion of "green revenues." In total just these three actions would produce in the United States over $7 trillion of "green revenues" during the next ten years. Think about how many jobs this would create for Americans.

So green is the answer businesses are looking for to spark consumer interest and purchases because:

1. *Your customers are thirsting to buy solutions that offer less cost, more meaning.*

2. *The size of the market is bigger than any other market segment you are targeting.*

Your Business and Investment Future

In summary, I wish I had a book like this in the 1980's explaining the future business opportunities tied to the microchip. I would have made a fortune because I would have been able to "see-forward" on how to invest in microchips and software technology.

This book offers that "see-forward" perspective on the Green Economic Revolution. This book provides the template on what is happening, why it is happening and how the pioneers in the Green Economic Revolution are making money growing green revenues.

In recognition that during these recessionary times many entrepreneurs and business people are attempting to conserve every dollar to meet payroll I am offering this introductory chapter for free. Just visit my website, http://www.earth2017.com, input your email address and the site will automatically email you back this chapter.

And in recognition that many of us don't have the time to wade through a thick book I have purposefully tried to keep it short by focusing upon the best practices of the companies I have interviewed who are building successful green businesses.

Finally, on my website are blogs, videos and links that provide current assessments on the opportunities being created by the Green Economic Revolution. Also, please check out the back of this book for the links that I use to follow the trends of the Green Economic Revolution.

Good luck in creating your recipe of *The Secret Green Sauce*™. I am looking forward to writing another book profiling the next generation of companies growing green revenues by:

1. Aligning Values with Value to create a competitive pricing strategy

2. Prove It, Conclusively! branding that provides the assurance needed to achieve market-leading brand equity

3. "Know It, Embrace It" marketing to grow revenues by engaging the Awareness Customer™ as they move along their path of learning, experimentation and then purchase of your green products that "cost less, mean more"!

Chapter One

The Economics
"Unsustainability": Costing More, Delivering Less

Much of the business world is still jaundiced about sustainability as a business path. Business people may want to "do good" but their fiduciary responsibility to their stockholders is to make money.

The key point that appears to get a business leader's attention is my documentation showing how sustainability's growth into a $10 trillion global market is NOT based upon "doing good." What I show them is that sustainability is a huge business opportunity based upon the economics. ***The mass adoption of sustainability is taking place because 20th Century business systems are increasingly costing more and delivering less.*** To paraphrase a Presidential campaign slogan on why sustainability will become a global path for revenue growth, "It's the economy, _____!"

The examples for why this is so are becoming increasingly obvious. In terms of the price at the pump who among us anticipates the price for gasoline will be 20% lower by 2017? NOTHING the oil industry can do will lower the price of gasoline. As a world we are awash in oil supply. The industry is pumping out record amounts of oil and they are doing a remarkable job of finding new oil fields in the most hostile of environments, political and physical. Yet, because the global demand for oil has increased to historically high levels as China and India join the United States as mega-consumers of oil, even in this global recession the price of oil is twice as high today compared to five years ago.

Who among us believe the price at the meter for electricity will decrease? The reality is that utilities across the country are filing for rate increases. The Energy Information Agency of the Department of Energy is projecting 3-4% *annual* increases in electricity prices. And utilities across the country are introducing Real Time Pricing, also known as Dynamic Pricing, tied to "smart meters" that can result in consumers paying prices during peak demand time periods that are 5 to 10 times higher than their average price per kWh. The facts are that the technology of central plant electricity production achieved its production efficiency ceiling in the 1970's. No technology improvement since then has changed the fact that basically this system is approximately 33% efficient meaning 67% of the energy in the fuel never reaches your meter.

And the industry's fuel costs to produce electricity are on an upward path. Today coal fuels 50% of our electricity generation. Many utilities are promoting "Clean Coal" as a technology to address the environmental impacts of coal-fueled electricity production that now accounts for 20% of the United States' total emission of greenhouse gases. Whether clean coal does emerge as a technology solution contributing to a solution to global warming and climate change is unclear. But one fact that is not in dispute is that clean coal electricity generation will not lower the price at the meter.

Natural gas is growing as the fuel alternative to coal. Natural gas is a lower emission alternative to coal but probably not a lower cost one (though the price of natural gas is at recent historical lows due to both the global recession, increased domestic supplies tied to advancements in drilling technology and increased supplies enabled by the development of a global liquefied natural gas transportation system).

And the electricity grid requires <u>billions</u> of dollars in upgrades and expansions. The utility industry is also spending <u>billions</u> of dollars on smart metering and information-connectivity. The reality is that sustainability in its many forms including conservation, energy efficiency, building efficiency, energy storage, renewable energy etc. is emerging as a competitively priced alternative to central generation, transmission-grid delivered and monopoly-supplied electricity.

Water is facing a similar collapse of "unsustainability." The agricultural-industrial complex is now confronting constraints upon its ability to consume water. California is a bread-basket for the United States and the world. But the State of California has grown to a size that current water supplies can no longer satisfy demand (and it appears Global Warming is reducing the supply of water stored in the form of snow during the winter on California's eastern mountain ranges). The impact upon the State's central valley of farms is water rationing and in some cases, a cut-off of supply. This same issue of allocating a limited supply of water is confronting one of America's fastest growing cities. Metropolitan Atlanta is confronting a requirement for massive water allocation reductions as a result of the states of Florida and Alabama winning a court injunction on Atlanta's access to the Chattahoochee River water system.

There is no technology that offers a *lower cost* solution to providing increased supplies of fresh water to California's farmers or Atlanta's citizens. The price for water supplied from rivers has to go up in recognition of its increased value (a classic case of economies where demand is exceeding supply and the process for achieving an equilibrium between supply and demand is a price increase that will reduce demand). Whether you have experienced it yet or not, expect the price at your water meter to be going up. And the least-cost solution to this higher price is a sustainable system for managing and using water supplies. (Bottle water is not a solution, costing more than the price per gallon for gasoline with a waste stream of 22 billion plastic bottles thrown away in America annually, an amount equal to 75 water bottles for every man, woman and child in America.)

The price of "unsustainability" is also surfacing in our food system. This is truly an amazing story of "Unintended Consequences" where a Presidential effort at eliminating hunger in America has resulted in record levels of obesity that is costing us billions in health care costs.

President Nixon established a target of eliminating hunger in America. He set this goal for his Secretary of Agriculture, Earl Butz. Secretary Butz went to the agriculture industry with this goal and their solution was mass production of corn and the introduction of corn fructose sugar as a staple ingredient in much of our food products. At this same time the emerging fast food and convenience food industries were looking for products to sell that were cheap, tasty and convenient. The result is history. We now have a mass production system supplying food that is cheap, tasty and convenient but that is also laced with sugar, starch, caffeine and cholesterol. The ramification is six out of ten Americans are overweight with 33% of American adults and 16% of our youth being obese. According to the Surgeon General's office one out of eight deaths are tied to obesity and beyond the loss of life this is placing a $117 billion annual cost upon our health care system. The Center for Disease Control (CDC) reports that only 33% of

Americans consumed two or more fruits per day and only 27% consumed vegetables three or more times a day. And included in the CDC's list of solutions is, in so many words, eating a sustainable diet that has much less fast food.

And the system of mass production of meat for our tasty diet is actually a major contributor to increased emissions of greenhouse gases. Cattle production accounts for 20% of the world's greenhouse gases. The source is the methane "released" by cattle. Today 33% of the world's land mass is dedicated to the production of cattle. Why? In 1950 the average American was eating 100 pounds of meat per year. Today we eat 185 pounds! Those "Big Mac's" add up in terms of pounds consumed, greenhouse gases emitted at the tail-end of cattle production (sorry for the pun, couldn't resist!) and in the increase of our cholesterol levels. (Ironically, our national cholesterol levels are at a modern historical low level but this result has been achieved through the dispensation of cholesterol-lowering pills to adults 60 years and older rather than from improved nutrition and increased exercise. **So if you are trying to figure out why we have high medical costs then remember this example where our diets have increased our cholesterol levels and rather than adopt a lower cost solution of proper nutrition we use the higher cost solution of ingesting medicines.**)

Housing and our transportation system is also collapsing in "unsustainability." Our housing sizes have doubled since the 1950's. The average post-war 1950's house was 983 sq. feet, by 1970 it was 1,500 sq. feet and today it is 2,345 per sq. feet.

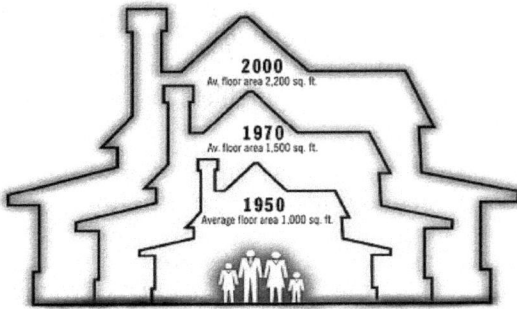

And this increase in housing size has occurred as the average household size has decreased from 3 in 1970 to 2.5 today. This means more space to heat and cool and more energy/water consumed per individual. This is not sustainable with increasing prices for energy and water and increasing environmental costs tied to emissions.

Our homes are also now located further from our places of employment creating increased commuting times with associated increases in fuel consumption and air emissions. Today the average American commute is 25 minutes. If you live in a major metropolitan area like NYC, Chicago or LA your commute is over thirty minutes. On average we spend 100 hours a year in our cars going to and from work. In total this represents 3.7 billion hours of time and 23 billion gallons of gasoline. This transportation system is collapsing under the weight of higher prices at the pump and the need to reduce greenhouse gas emissions.

And once we arrive at work we enter buildings that are often energy hogs. The Green Building Council estimates that our offices consume 70% of the electricity consumed in the United States. And these offices account for 38% of all greenhouse gas emissions with a growth rate of emissions that is faster than any other sector.

Food, energy, water, health care, housing, transportation, the 20th Century's business systems are experiencing a collapse of "unsustainability" as their value decreases in terms of our health, our environment's health and our financial well-being.

And this is happening on a global scale.

The non-profit Water For People reports that approximately 1 billion people in the world do not have access to clean water and 2.5 billion lack adequate sanitation. What does that mean on a human level? Every day 5,000 babies in the world die due to a lack of clean water. This is unacceptable. It is also unsustainable to think in this world of connectivity that a billion people will accept this type of infant mortality while we flush perfectly clean drinking water down our commodes and use it to irrigate our lawns. In fact, a world survey of a representative sample of 1,000 people in each of 15 countries including the United States, Canada, China, India, Mexico and Russia that was conducted by the Circle of Blue/GlobeScan and funded by Molson Coors Brewing Company found that 90% of those polled "...expressed a conviction that access to clean, fresh water is fundamental, not only for themselves but for all people."

The world's oceans are facing collapse from unsustainable fishing and pollution. Dead zones are emerging offshore in response to human action. (A dead zone is an oxygen depletion that kills marine life.) The Gulf of Mexico has an approximately 7,000 sq. mile dead zone which is about the size of New Jersey.

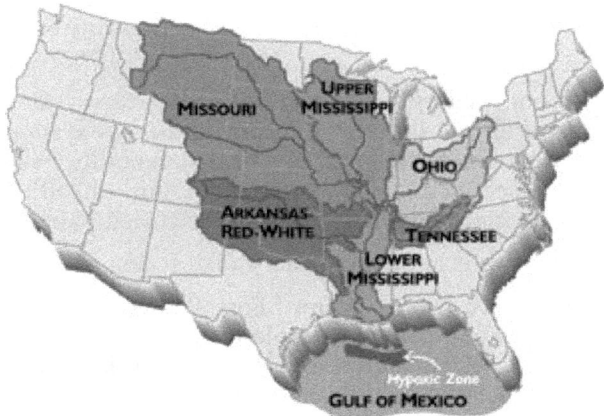

Picture located at www.ers.usda.gov

Scientific research is pointing to nitrogen dumped into the Gulf from farm runoff that flows through the Mississippi River into the Gulf as the source cause for this dead zone. The nitrogen accelerates the growth of algae and plankton which, when it dies and sinks to the Gulf's floor, decays in a manner that extracts oxygen from the water. And this loss of oxygen is large enough that it is killing the Gulf's marine life on a massive scale. And the reason this scientific research is pointing toward our agricultural system is because two-thirds of the nitrogen in the Mississippi River comes from farm runoff of chemical fertilizers and the manure on agricultural lands.

The coastal waters off of Oregon and Washington also have dead zones. Marine ecologists at Oregon State University published a study in the journal *Science* that reported a massive killing of floor dwelling crabs and other marine life and their research pointed to Global Warming. One of the ramifications of Global Warming due to human emission of Greenhouse Gases is the acidification of the oceans as they absorb increasingly massive amounts of CO_2.

Overfishing is compounding this stress upon our ocean. 90% of such key dietary fish like tuna, cod, marlin, swordfish and flounder have reached or have approached the status of "fished-out" since the introduction of industrial fishing with its hugely efficient systems for locating, harvesting, processing and storing fish on sophisticated ships that work in fleets. The result is a massive decline in supply and a corresponding increase in price. One example of this system's collapse was the demise of the cod fishery off Newfoundland and the attendant loss of approximately 40,000 jobs. California's fishing industry is facing a similar crisis as the fail in the annual salmon run has resulted in government imposed restrictions that have basically stopped commercial fishing. According to the United Nation's Food and Agriculture Organization six percent of all major marine fisheries are under exploited, 20% are moderately exploited, 50% are fully exploited, 15% are overfished, 6% are depleted and only 2% are recovering. If you add these percentages the result is that over 70% of our world's fisheries are "fully exploited, overfished or depleted."

Not Alarmist, Business Opportunity

The purpose behind this chapter is not to be alarmist. Rather, the purpose of this brief analysis is to highlight that the 20th Century's systems are now costing consumers more and delivering less value. *This is the recipe for a massive business opportunity on a global scale.* And this opportunity is consumer driven.

Every consumer market segment is in play as consumers aggressively seek business/product alternatives to:

- Continued price escalation of unsustainable 20th Century products

- Increases in public taxes/debt to pay for the consequential costs of Global Warming and global geo-political unrest tied to "unsustainability" and,

- Increasing individual insurance premiums to pay for a health care system that is approaching a tipping point of financial "unsustainability."

The strategic business opportunity being created by "unsustainability" is nothing less than a revolution. But this is not a revolution for "doing good" (though thankfully many of the early "revolutionaries" were motivated by morals, ethics and a desire to serve a greater purpose than their self-interest).

This is not a government inspired or driven revolution. Yes, governments around the world are introducing new laws and regulations that address the consequences of the 20th Century's collapsing systems. But the key point is that government actions are in reaction to a problem and not a stimulus for change.

What this is not is a repeat of the 1970's "Corporate Responsibility" movement where great efforts were made to link a profit incentive to acting responsibly toward the environment and minorities. Rather, *this is a pure shift in the economics that is now tilting competitive advantage toward businesses adopting sustainability as a strategic core of their competitive strategy*.

The stimulus for change is squarely centered upon the consumer and the business competitor. The consumer is seeking less cost, more meaning. **And the ramifications within a free market system are that either existing businesses will meet consumer expectations or face new or increasing competition from businesses and entrepreneurs who see the opportunity.** And what this book outlines are the stories of businesses and entrepreneurs who are winning new revenues because they are offering consumers sustainable goods and services that cost less and mean more.

Right now much of the competitive response to change by legacy companies offering 20th Century solutions is increased lobbying. That is actually a great "bull-market" sign for entrepreneurs pursuing sustainable solutions. Here's the logic for such optimism. Why would a legacy 20th Century company invest millions in lobbying if they have the ability to offer consumers lower cost, more meaning? The energy industry (oil, coal and utility companies) has spent $80 million in 90 days lobbying on the proposed legislation to introduce a Cap and Trade system for pricing at the pump and meter the environmental cost created from emitting greenhouse gases. And this lobbying has dramatically impaled the legislation's initial purpose. But ultimately, will this prevent consumers from buying renewable energy solutions or will it dampen their interest in technologies that lower bills through efficiency gains if renewable energy and energy efficiency technologies are price competitive compared to the escalating prices and environmental costs of utility supplied, fossil-fuel generated electricity?

The health care industry has spent $160 million in 90 days lobbying on the health care legislation. Why would they if they had a path to offer consumers lower price alternatives that produced improved health? But the reality is that today's health-care system is collapsing under the weight of a cost-plus vs. performance-based pricing model that is being fed a growing number of customers by our culture defined by fast foods and lifestyles based upon the car rather than exercise. But encouragingly, businesses and entrepreneurs are developing sustainable, lower cost solutions.

In summary, *this is the business opportunity of a lifetime* because the 20th Century market leaders are collapsing under their weight of "unsustainability" and in many cases their strategy is to attempt to slow or stop the consumer's path toward lower cost, more meaning alternative products. This is opening the door for the companies and entrepreneurs profiled in this book to grow revenues selling sustainability. As you will read in the profiles of these companies and entrepreneurs it doesn't matter if your core business is based upon a price-driven commodity like office supplies or your business is as small as a local retail store. The collapse of "unsustainability" is creating business opportunities in every market and market segment in the United States and the world.

The BUSINESS DRIVERS for success within the Green Economic Revolution are:

- ***Price-competitiveness*** compared to 20th Century solutions that are collapsing under their own weight of higher prices that deliver less customer satisfaction

- **A consumer focus** aligned with and enabling the consumer's self-educating process on sustainability including what to buy and who to buy from

- ***Establishing credibility*** for your company and your product compared to the greenwashing Band-Aids being applied to 20th Century goods and services that are not sustainable in terms of their future economics and their impacts upon the environment and human wellness.

And the companies that are growing green revenues are using these tools:

1. Aligning Value with Values to achieve a pricing strategy that grows in its competitiveness as less sustainable competitors confront consumers with price increases

2. Using "Prove it, Conclusively" branding to assure the consumer that what they are buying aligns with the consumer's sustainability expectations in terms of the product and the company

3. Engaging their customers in a "Know it, Embrace it" outreach process that engages them in the discovery of solutions that ""cost less, mean more"."

"The Secret Green Sauce"

Chapter Two

Market Research
Awareness Customer™

A new customer has emerged that is leading the Green Economic Revolution. I call this unique market segment the Awareness Customer™. The Awareness Customer™ is defined by their:

- Proactive awareness on the need for change developed through self-education

- Engagement in one or more related change-processes

- Early procurement-adoption of sustainable goods and services.

And the size of the "green" market segment is large and growing. **Today 85% of Americans have purchased a green product**. A Google search of the words "green product" produces 1.6 *billion* hits!

The speed in which consumers have shifted toward buying green is historically unprecedented. JD Powers and Associates conducts ongoing surveys of "web-conversations" to track consumer trends. One area they have been tracking is sustainability. In 2007 their survey found that 56% of web-conversations were "debating the issue" of sustainability. In 2009 their survey found that 68% of web-conversations *were debating the solution*! In other words the focus is upon what to buy and who to buy from.

According to JD Powers and Associates this is an unprecedented shift both in terms of scale and speed. What the JD Powers and Associates' findings suggest is that the debate is over.

The Awareness Customer™ has decided change is required and is seeking sustainable businesses and products that _offer less cost and more meaning_.

Additional supporting market research evidence on the emergence of the Awareness Customer™ includes:

- Even in the face of this recession, an annual survey called the ImagePower Green Brands developed by Cohn & Wolfe, Landor Associates, Esty Environmental Partners and Penn, Schoen & Berland, found that *76% of consumers expect to spend the same or more on green products.* (And this same survey found this to be an international trend where 73 percent of Chinese consumers, 78 percent of Indians and 73 percent of Brazilians say they will spend more on green.)

- A published study by Miller Zell, Inc (a leader in retail strategy design) found that 62% of consumers said that green product options will influence their *unplanned* purchases.

- A study commissioned by the Grocery Manufacturer's Association (GMA) found that "...while sustainable product attributes are not the dominant purchasing driver for the majority of consumers, they tend to be a tie-breaker when price and performance are in parity."

How motivated are consumers in their search for sustainability? The Miller Zell study found that 50% of consumers are willing to pay more for green! Let this last sentence sink in for a second. How many customers of yours are willing to pay more? Potentially 50% of them if they see you and your products as being the sustainable solutions they are searching for.

The Awareness Customer™ is actually three groups of consumer leaders. Each is distinctive. Each has their own definition of sustainability and their own performance metrics for what it means to be sustainable. But combined, these three groups account for over $10 trillion in annual purchases and they are actively engaged in shifting their purchases toward businesses and products that sell sustainability.

CONCERNED CAREGIVERS:
$8.5 Billion Powerhouse

The first group of green consumer leaders is Concerned Caregivers. It's our moms. They see sustainability as a path to protect and enhance their family's well being. Many Concerned Caregivers use the term "Wellness" when talking about sustainability.

Diane MacEachern Founder/CEO of the Big Green Purse is an expert on women buying behaviors and most especially Concerned Caregivers. She is so perceptive and informed about how women behave (including their interactions with men) that every time I have heard her talk I come away thinking she has some type of window into my family and the dynamics between me, my wife and my daughter. In a speech she gave before the Sustainable Brands 09 conference she noted that 85% of consumer purchases are made by women! *I estimate this be $8.5 trillion in annual buying power.* And Diane is seeing an increasing shift in Concerned Caregivers' buying power toward businesses and products that protect their loved ones and enhance their family's future.

One major focus of the Concerned Caregiver is upon diet and health. They are buying organic foods. Because they are seeking a lower cost for healthy foods they are engaging in home and community gardening. (This also aligns with their passion for a communal experience of working and harvesting within a network of women.) They are strong supporters of farmer markets. They are the major reason the New Oxford Dictionary selected "Locavore" (a person who eats locally produced and prepared food) as its word of the year.

Concerned Caregivers are also researching the health impacts of the chemicals in their homes. They are experimenting with purchases of products like Green Works and Seventh Generation and in many cases shifting to these more sustainable products. They are looking to upgrade their home's air indoor quality out of health concerns for their loved ones and are now sensitized to the chemical emissions in their home's carpets, cabinets and paints. They are trying compact fluorescent lights as a way to both reduce their family's expenditure on electricity and as a way to improve the environment for their kids (though many still have issues with the quality of the lighting). Synovate, a global market research company, published a study that found American homeowners largest percentage of focus on "greening" their homes is upon energy efficiency (45%), "energy and atmosphere" (26%) and "environmentally friendly material" (20%). They are also looking for automobiles that satisfy their need to haul their family around, to commute cost-effectively to work and that align with their growing sense that we need cleaner cars because today's auto emissions are harmful to their loved ones.

CEOs:
Setting numerical performance targets

The second group of green consumers is the Corporate CEO. Yes, the target of much wrath from environmentalists is increasingly leading the charge in reducing CO_2 emissions. The facts are that many corporate CEOs of Fortune 500 companies now view global warming as being a creation of human activity and the source-cause for damaging climate change. They see themselves as having the power to affect change and stop Global Warming. And today, the majority of Fortune 500 companies have are now measuring their carbon footprints and many have begun to set enterprise-scale CO_2 emission reduction goals, typically a 20% reduction by 2020.

And this is hugely important based upon original research conducted by Oregon State University Professor JunJie Wu that was published in the Journal of Environmental Management. My take on Professor Wu's study is that aligning with consumers, investors and interest groups on sustainability does not become a goal of Corporate America unless the CEO establishes it as a strategic goal (interestingly, it appears that privately owned companies are more likely to adopt sustainability than a large, public corporation, a finding I share from my anecdotal experience).

And for those companies embracing the strategic goal of reducing their carbon footprint the use of "Green Teams" has gained common acceptance as an effective tool for change. Green teams are typically work associate empowered groups that are organized to identify CO_2

emission-reducing solutions. And of all the officers below the CEO who are embracing the Green Team initiative it is the CFO. They are seeing the results where cutting CO_2 emissions typically also result in cost reductions that flow straight to the company's bottom line.

A personal favorite story about a green team is one that was formed in the IT department of an international bank. The Senior VP over this organization believes that Global Warming is a major threat to humanity and decided to explore how his department could contribute toward reducing CO_2 emissions. He found his vision was shared by many of his work associates in the U.S. office. They organized a team (they didn't know to call it a green team) and began to figure out the basic "how-to" first steps like calculating their carbon footprint, rank ordering activities by the size of their emissions and brainstorming ideas for reducing CO_2 emissions. And they were, like most green teams, successful. They found ways to reduce their operation's CO_2 footprint. And their success migrated via the grapevine within the IT organization resulting in voluntary green teams starting up in their international locations. What is cool about this pioneering effort is that one day a representative from the CFO's office called upon the Senior VP to inquire why IT costs were going down! A longer story made shorter, this international bank now has CO_2 emissions as an element in their strategic mission, has assigned a senior officer to the role of Chief Sustainability Officer and they are realizing cost savings that are contributing toward the bank's profitability. They also have set up a "for-profit" department focused upon making business loans on renewable energy projects and to fund their client's investments in energy efficiency.

A related story comes from a smaller firm that tried its first green team. It was a collection of about a dozen volunteers. As is typical, the group did identify and implement ideas for reducing the carbon footprint of the company. And by so doing, they also created documentable cost savings. But an unanticipated result was a change in the personal behavior of the green team's members. They are now "greening their lives" When I interviewed the team members about their green team they were most enthusiastic about how their own sense of awareness had increased with a resulting impact upon how they lived and shopped. Each had one or more individual examples of what they were now doing to go green. One of the ironies I am seeing played out across companies where the CEOs have adopted reducing CO_2 emissions as a strategic goal is an unintended consequence of creating Awareness Customers™ out of the participating green team members.

MILLENIALS:
Their future

The Millennial Generation (those born between 1977 and 1986) is the third group of green consumer leaders. There are 70 million Millennials. There numerical size is 90% the Boomer Generation's size and they hold in their numerical size the same potential the Boomer Generation exerted in revolutionizing America's social and consumption patterns. And they are economically motivated. While better educated they are earning less than their parents at the same age. They are burdened with college tuition debt. They are just entering their years of employment and peak earning years with a sense they have to come up with a business model that offers them more income potential than being offered by 20th Century's corporations and financial systems. It is

43

this generation that will be determining America's economic and environmental future.

Increasingly they see inheriting a future from their parents that is less healthy, with geo-political risks tied to the 20th Century business systems' focus upon harvesting increasingly scarce natural resources and with diminished financial opportunity as more of the economy's productivity has to be paid for the costs of systems collapsing into "unsustainability." Because they see their future threatened if there is not a massive shift into sustainability, this is the one group most willing to pay more for green goods and services. The Miller Zell survey found that 62% of Millennials were willing to pay more for green products.

And they see green as "cool" (one of their key definitional words). To them green is an iPod. It is Twitter. They see green as the new "black" because it goes with everything. It is what they wear, how they live and how they envision making their living. Green is an integral part of their communal world of connectivity that enables frictionless interaction with their peers that build honesty/trust, offers a personal touch and the ability to customize what they buy and what they do based upon their individual participation/inputs. In terms of their procurement decisions it is their sense of the future, lifestyle issues and peer opinion that are stronger influence drivers on their consumption decisions than price.

And they embrace the concept of a "Starfish" organization where the community centers its creative efforts upon a topic or issue. In music their "starfish" focus is "sharing" to achieve personalized and low cost customized play lists. They embraced Napster and migrated to iTunes to avoid the legal prosecution tied to downloading copy-righted material. But the key point is their actions revolutionized the music industry. It empowered a new industry leader in Apple selling billions of iTunes. And the Millennial Generation's collective actions achieved ""cost less, mean more"" by replacing carbon-based CD plastic and its packaging waste stream through the digitization of music distribution.

They also have embraced Craigslist. The result (whether for the better is to be seen) is the decline and anticipated demise of the local newspaper. Now ads are digitized. And so is the news. And it is free. Plus, it can be customized by such tools as a "MyYahoo" page. It can be delivered daily through a wireless network via Kindle or Net-books. Now the Millennial Generation is pushing out the old system of buying books at college book stores by substituting down loading them onto Kindle. The result for them is a lower cost for books and for our environment, a dramatically reduced consumption of physical resources tied to the production, transportation and distribution of books Millennials are leading the technology charge to achieve ""cost less, mean more"!"

"Cost less, Mean more"

"Cost less, Mean more", is the mantra of the Awareness Customer™. While these four words convey the passion of their mission their collective actions actually consist of the following six key expectations:

1. *Something anyone can do.* We are all one big "Green Team." Adopting sustainability should be like shopping or advertising on "Craigslist" in terms of the ease in figuring out what works for an individual that collectively works for our planet and our fellow human beings. And on a collective basis, enabled by Web 2.0, it is a "starfish behavior process" where the

group comes together upon the common task to affect sustainable change. Today, Web 2.0 is exploding with starfish networks on community gardening, solar power, health impacts of chemicals, Chinese toys with lead, etc., etc., etc. Engagement is the 'street-name-location' where green is sold.

2. *ZERO added cost, in fact it should be lower in cost.* So rather than pay $20 for a CD and then having to throw away the packaging it should be as easy as down-loading individual tunes for 99 cents that can be listened to across a range of digital technologies and locations. It is the roof-top solar power retailers who are financing the product's installation by offering their customers a payment system of zero-down-payment and monthly payments that are at least equal if not lower than the monthly savings on the customer's electricity bill achieved by substituting solar power for utility-supplied power. It is Honda offering the first "under $20,000" four-passenger hybrid automobile.

3. *Can be easily implemented.* This shouldn't be rocket science. It should be as easy as buying a cup of coffee, except the coffee should be certified as being produced from farms that are acting in a sustainable manner regarding the environment and their work associates. It is as easy as waking up in the morning and reading Tweets, or getting on Facebook or reading the Wall Street Journal that your Kindle automatically downloaded while you were sleeping.

4. *High positive impacts.* "Live long and prosper." It is a sustainable system that replaces extraction, and even recycling, with restoration. It is "cradle-to-cradle" product design. These are solutions that solve our addiction to foreign oil, free us from dependency upon a health care system that is too expensive and

exclusive, that restores our global business competitiveness and most importantly to the future, restores the health of our environment. Need a supporting statistic to be convinced on where the Awareness Customer™ is heading toward? How about the market survey result that shows 71% of Americans want manufacturers to take back their products at the end of their useful lives.

5. *Be real*. Businesses, green-wash at your own risk! The classic example comes from a speech I was giving where I outlined the water bottle industry's efforts at coming up with a more sustainable plastic bottle. A woman in the front row (a classic Concerned Caregiver) raises her hand and asks, "What's sustainable about a plastic bottle?" Action, not hype, is the expectation the Awareness Customer™ is establishing as the standard for who they will be doing business with. For example, 80+% of Americans want the geographic origin of food to be placed on the food label, and they want those labels to have facts they can readily understand, for the facts to be informative and for them to be real!

6. *Real change, now*. Despite those who still don't believe, the Awareness Customer™ hears a ticking bomb tied to our legacy 20th Century business systems producing irreversible harm to our plant and their lives. They believe the scale of the problem and the limited amount of time left to create solutions requires the immediate re-engineering of business systems. For a legacy 20th Century company this looks like a threat to their survival and a revolution that should be lobbied against. Such actions will not keep the Awareness Customer™ from searching for both the politicians and the businesses that can implement real change, now.

The fundamental 21st Century strategic business question every company now faces is:

"How to align with the Awareness Customer™."

Achieving such an alignment will create an opportunity to win market share in this emerging $10 trillion global market. Not doing so runs the risk of creating disloyal customers that can threaten your business's profitability and eventually its survival.

And the path for doing so consists of the following three basic steps:

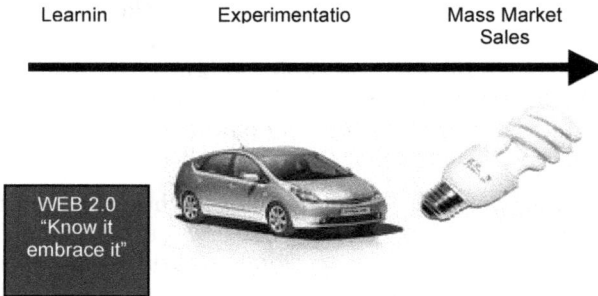

The remaining chapters of this book will provide best practices being used by successful green businesses that are deploying "Know it, Embrace it," experimentation and mass marketing to grow green revenues.

Chapter Three

Pricing
Aligning Value and Values

I have a lot of friends in the home construction business. As I write this book these are very tough times for the home construction industry trying to absorb a financing debacle. Many of my friends in this business are surviving by selling green. But even among these green builders they hold a very jaundiced frustration toward the customer. As one green builder summarized to me, "As soon as I say it costs more the typical customer stops wanting to build a green home."

Why isn't this surprising? The fact that amazes and encourages me is that there are a significant number of customers who are paying more to go green. But for sustainability to grow beyond a niche market sustainable goods and services have to become competitive in price.

Here's a quote I share with the many green-entrepreneurs who are not being successful balancing economics and the environment:

> ***"75% of people that buy a hybrid,***
> ***do it for economic reasons, not environmental."***
> J.D. Powers and Associates

First Base Is Price!

One of the key entrepreneur-lessons I facilitate for my clients is answering this question:

"How are you going to get to first base?"

Implied in this question are these two key issues:

1. Which way to first base?
2. What is "first base?"

I can not tell you how many businesses and entrepreneurs don't have realistic and effective answers when I ask this question. They can tell me where home is located because that is their vision of success. They can tell me what second and third base looks like because that is their growth expectations. But getting to first base is the first step in rounding the bases. And the "first base" that too many companies fail to achieve is a pricing strategy that 1)defines how to win early-adopter customers and 2)migrate from this initial success onto continuous price improvements that will achieve price leadership. What typically happens for companies with out a "Crossing the Green-Price Chasm™" is some initial sale success from that smaller market segment of green consumers who will pay more to be green and then the green-business hits a revenue wall because they can't lower their prices to attract a broader range of customers and/or successfully face a competitive price challenger.

The idea of building a business selling sustainability without having a clearly articulated price competitiveness strategy is a recipe for failure. An effective pricing strategy has a "point of entry" that will engage the "first base" early adopter customer AND a path for gaining/achieving mass marketing price competitiveness.

In terms of selling green there are two ways to design such a strategy. One is to anticipate the increasing price of "unsustainability" outlined in Chapter One. "Unsustainability" makes the path toward achieving pricing parity for sustainability easier as the price of "unsustainability" increases. This is a "waiting for a falling star" pricing strategy.

But waiting for the collapse of "unsustainability" to price itself to parity with sustainability is fraught with risk. It also does not address the growing sense of urgency being felt by the Awareness Customer™. **The growth opportunity is having a business path for being a leader in offering ""cost less, mean more".**"

And there are companies selling sustainability that have successfully achieved price parity or even price leadership. And the result for these companies is explosive growth and increased market share.

My favorite example is Give Something Back run by two great entrepreneurs, Sean Marx (CEO) and Mike Hannigan (President). They sell office supplies. This is an approximately $200 billion annual revenue industry that is characterized by intense price competition and where the largest competitor only has 10% market share. "Much of our revenues come from winning blind-bids where lowest price is the determining procurement factor," explains Mike. And yet in this highly price competitive market segment Give Something Back averages selling about 60-80% recycled paper compared to an industry standard of about 10%. And they have grown their business to a scale where they are now the largest independent office supply company in Northern California and they are now expanding into the rest of California and other states. They are "Example A" of the revenue potential for businesses that can align with the

Awareness Customer's™ search for ""cost less, mean more"."

And because of their customer/sustainability focus they keep finding new ways for growing revenues and aligning with their customers' needs. For example, daily they deliver supplies via delivery trucks. These trucks used to come back to their warehouse empty. Now they have the delivery trucks pick up the boxes delivered previously for recycling. This lowers the customer's waste disposal costs. And it lowers Give Something Back's cost of packaging as now about 20% of their packaging consists of reused boxes. At the time of this book's writing Give Something Back has begun expanding the service to include a pick up of the customer's e-wastes!

Apple is a classic example of a company that is so focused upon its customers that it is pioneering sustainability not because Steve Jobs' established this as management goal but rather, as a result of their product innovation focus. Apple's digitizing of consumer entertainment and information services is a classic example for how to "align value with values." They created price leadership on buying music and other services they call "Apps". Today consumers can create their music inventory at 99 cents per song. And they can buy specialized application services for their phones that include an ever growing range of services including help on writing school papers, finding restaurants and calculating mortgage payments at prices that range between free to a couple of dollars. An obvious sustainability result is a massive reduction in packaging, paper and transportation with all of the associated CO_2 emissions and waste-stream reductions. *But the key point is that Apple's design success is not an environmental "thing" but rather a customer satisfaction path for achieving competitive advantage through aligning value with values.* Apple's designs are generating cool products, great prices, increased revenues, higher stock valuations <u>and lower emissions</u>. *"cost less, mean more"!*

The roof top solar power industry is another example. The cost for energy from a roof top solar system is almost 100% the upfront cost of the solar panels, installation costs and related costs for interties with the electricity company's system. (After the system is installed the typical operations and maintenance cost is a periodic cleaning of the solar panels to remove surface dust, bird droppings, etc.) In addition, it is financially difficult for most electricity consumers to pay upfront for the equivalent of 20+ years of electricity supply. Therefore, in the early history of selling roof top solar systems the sales process was limited to the few customers who could afford to pay $10-20,000 upfront for a 20 plus year supply of practically "free" electricity. But the industry has figured this out. Today customers have a number of paths for buying a solar roof top system with no money down and even guarantees by the solar company that the savings on the electricity bill will cover the monthly payment. So in these programs aligning value with values results for the customer are lower monthly payments compared to their old electricity bills, protection against future utility price-increases by "fixing" the price through the installation of a solar generating system and when the system is paid off, having a solar power system that is producing "free" electricity with zero CO_2 emissions. ""cost less, mean more"."

Renova Energy Corporation is a company located in Palm Desert, California that has a very well thought-out "get to first base" pricing strategy. Their business goal is to sell roof top solar systems. However, roof top solar's high investment cost for commercial and residential customers is a barrier to them buying solar. To overcome this pricing barrier Renova has developed what I call a "good, better, best" pricing path.

Their "good" price is free! (Free always sell, EVERY business should have a "free" product offering to engage and build trust with a customer.) Renova's free product is an energy audit. The audit builds trust with the customer by showing Renova's technical expertise and it engages the customer by surfacing scenarios where hiring Renova satisfies some value need of the customer.

The "better" priced offerings are a range of lower cost, high payback, energy efficiency actions that will lower the building's operating cost while also increasing its comfort. These lower cost action items can include solar attic fans (very clever, proving the technology's value to the customer on a lower initial cost application), tinted windows, solar tubes (bringing inside a building the natural light that offers a softer, natural lighting experience with no electricity costs), installing LED lighting and enhancing the thermal dynamics of the roof by installing a "cool" roof or radiant barrier (this is Palm Desert so their focus is upon keeping a building from growing internal heat levels to levels that are uncomfortable and uneconomic).

Renova's "best" price is a solar system. It is "best" because it builds upon the prior price offerings tied to energy efficiency that have successfully lowered the size, and therefore the investment required, for a solar system that can either eliminate very high priced peak power from the utility or move the customer to a net zero energy result that holds the potential zeroing out their electric bill from the utility. And by sizing the unit to displace the utility electricity supplied during the highest price time periods which often is also when the sun is shining they can increase the payback attractiveness of the system for their customers.

The reason I went through all these steps of explanation is that Renova is surviving in a very difficult recession/depression market for home/commercial construction because they have a well-thought out pricing plan that still engages their target customers and is still generating revenues. "*"cost less, mean more""* is a pricing path for both revenue growth and *revenue survival.*

How To Align Value With Values

The strategic issue facing every business is how to become a price leader in sustainability?

Geoffrey A. Moore's pioneering marketing book *"Crossing The Chasm"* is a model for this pricing future. The basic premise of Moore's book is that the successful introduction of a new technology is similar to the Normandy Invasion during WWII where you first have to establish a "beachhead" before you can win the war. In the case of price leadership in sustainability the strategic issue is what is your Crossing the Green Pricing Chasm™ beachhead from which to grow into a market leader that delivers less cost, more meaning? I call this "Aligning Value with Values."

Many pioneering green companies are now hitting their "revenue-wall" due to their strategic focus upon, "What is the environmental benefit to be achieved?" They achieved initial revenue success because there are Awareness Customers who will pay more for sustainable solutions. But now these companies are facing a leveling off, or a decline in revenues, because they don't have a pricing path for selling more to more people and/or they don't have a pricing solution when their competitors (which can include legacy 20th Century companies who are starting to sell green) begin to offer competitive prices.

While a values-focus is admirable, the more effective *business focus* is:

> *"How can price leadership be achieved that will produce sustainable and growing revenues?"*

See the difference in perspective? **The business strategy that begins with aligning value** to targeted *values* has a path to high revenue volume and market share leadership.

First Solar is a classic example of how the combination of a Crossing the Green Pricing Chasm strategy and economies of scale can create a high growth business opportunity. The solar industry's vision is the $1 per watt solar panel which they estimate can achieve price parity with electric utility supplied electricity. When I first met First Solar in 2004 they were a cost leader among solar manufacturers with a cost of around $2-2.50 per watt. They had identified an Awareness Customer beachhead in Europe and California for customers who, typically subsidized by government programs, were buying solar systems. But First Solar never took their eye off the target of gaining pricing parity with utility grid supplied electricity. First Solar announced on February 25, 2009 that they achieved a $1 per watt manufacturing cost. Their current manufacturing capacity is now approximately 1,000 MWs or an amount about equal in size to a typically sized nuclear power plant. First Solar has gained market share leadership in solar power by achieving pricing leadership and their stock has increased in value by almost 500% since 2005! And they continue to use economies of scale to create price leadership from growing their revenues. Today First Solar projects the ability to manufacture a solar watt of power at less than 90 cents.

We have been here before in the history of technology. When the microprocessor was first introduced it was a niche gizmo appealing only to a select few exploring something they called a PC. Gradually, mass market uses were found for the microchip like the infamous Hewlett Packard hand-held calculator and then the "Pong" video game that captured the consumer's imagination with a simple game of table tennis. The rest, of course, is history. Today we use over 100 micro-processors to run our daily lives. Without even thinking about it we depend upon the microchip for everything from managing our car's performance on the way to work to watching TV at the end of the work day. Microchip prices are the classic example of economies of scale where larger scale production and advancements along the learning curve continuously drive prices lower and increase the breadth and quality of microchip-enabled consumer products.

This is the path sustainability has now started down. *We are at a "Macintosh" point of time* in terms of sustainability's position on the path of economies of scale. Soon sustainability will have its own infamous commercial like the one Apple launched introducing the Macintosh during the 1984 Super Bowl ad by announcing "1984 won't be like 1984." My vision of that **green** milestone "Super Bowl Ad" will be something like this, "Costs less, Means more."

Crossing The Green Pricing Chasm™

The first step in determining "value" is to define the price target. In First Solar's case their goal was to be the solar manufacturer to achieve $1 per watt. For Apple Computer's sale of iTunes it was the 99 cents song. For Give Something Back it was a business strategy that had at its core the requirement of being price competitive in a bid process.

To achieve price leadership you have to define the price target taking into account competitive challenges. Few companies can launch their green product or service as a price leader. But the successful ones know what it takes to be a price leader and they have a strong plan for achieving this result in the face of anticipated price competition.

A typical milestone event in a Crossing the Green Pricing Chasm™ is pricing parity where the green solution has the same price or budget amount as the "unsustainable" competitive alternative. My wife's business is an example of applying Align Value with Values to win new business offering price parity for green solutions.

She is an interior decorator. Her business is consulting to clients looking to remodel their home or office. Her deliverable is identifying products and vendors that fulfilled the visual expectations and budgets of her clients. She sells "sizzle" but this is still a price driven, and highly competitive, business. So what she really is selling is "sizzle" at the customer's budget and using her expertise, lowering the customer's risk of a poor result.

She is now gaining competitive advantage and winning bids by deploying the process of aligning value with values in offering green solutions. She still begins every sales opportunity with a discovery process where my wife asks the potential client to outline what they want to achieve and how much they want to spend (sometimes the architect attempts to speak for the customer but she is persistent in wanting to hear this in the customer's own words). Interestingly, often the first statement from the potential client is "We have so many dollars of budget to spend." Doesn't that make sense? The customer understands this is an optimization process of trying to gain as much value as their budget allows. They don't begin with values, they begin with value and work toward the "amount" of values their budget can pay for.

What has now changed in my wife's business practice is she now asks, "What are your health and lifestyle goals?" Surprisingly, more and more of her customers (many are Concerned Caregivers) have a specific health goal for their remodeling. The classic example was a family with an asthmatic child. My wife won this $600,000 contract because her bid was not only a great design within their target budget but it also identified solutions for reducing the chemical air emissions tied to the home remodeling that held the potential of improving indoor air quality, a huge benefit for a family with an asthmatic child. Only a few years ago this was not even on the list of deliverables of what an interior decorator would think about proposing and today it is a key source of revenue for my wife's business. She is winning bids because she is a price leader on providing "*sustainable sizzle.*" Her remodeling projects are visually stunning. Her prices are within the client's budget. And she offers more meaning by satisfying the Concerned Caregiver's needs, whether it's a healthier indoor air quality or therapeutic tubs for their spouse's bad back or increased charm through the use of recycled materials or lower utility bills.

Canyon Construction and Diefenbach Development use similar aligning value with values strategies for selling green. Canyon Construction invested in building a platinum LEED certified headquarters building. They use the building to engage perspective clients on the environmental and cost effectiveness for going green. They can walk a perspective through the building showing how water capture systems can lower water bills and reduce damaging run-off into our water systems. They can show them solar panels that look like roof tiles that supplement much of the building's need for electricity, reducing their electric bill. They can show them gardens with native shrubs that are truly beautiful and with lower maintenance cost for fertilizers, weeding and water compared to gardens using non-native plants.

Marty Diefenbach, President of Dienfenbach Development loves well-engineered technologies (and his passion is owning and fixing up Porsches). He has licensed a wall technology that is cheaper to install than the traditional wood framing systems, can withstand hurricane force winds and dramatically reduces the operating time of a building's heating and cooling systems because of the wall structure's insulation and air penetration advantages compared to the best wood framed walls. He also offers the latest in smart home wiring and technologies. But the key point is that in his bids he has to be price competitive. He is selling green but his pricing has to be competitive against non-green competitors. That's doesn't mean he wins every bid because going green is still not the least cost path, yet, but he has a strategy to be price competitive and this strategy is enabling his business survival during this home construction depression.

An example of a strategy that is not working is web-based retailing of green. In 2006 I did a considerable amount of strategy work on the potential for selling green via the web. On first analysis the idea of green merchants selling through the Internet appeared to be an obviously exciting opportunity. The size of the opportunity appeared large in anticipation of Millennial Generation and Concern Caregiver consumers using the web to find their green products. And it was anticipated that selling via the web with its lower carbon footprint compared to a physical store would be highly compelling to the Awareness Customer™. But so far there have been many high-quality start-ups but no break-through successes. The reason for this lack of success is that none of the competitors created a ""cost less, mean more"" impression upon the Awareness Customer™ compared to the traditional retailers.

The missed strategic-dynamic was a competitive threat from big box retailers like Walmart, The Home Depot and Lowe's selling sustainable products at competitive prices. Walmart is now a global leader in selling sustainability. In 2006 they began to sell organic foods in the food section of their stores. They have just announced a plan to have every product they sell ranked by a sustainability index.

To a lesser degree, other big box retailers like The Home Depot and Lowes have also embraced sustainability by offering energy efficient lights and appliances. For example, The Home Depot gave away 1 million CFL (Compact Florescent Light) light bulbs on Earth Day in 2007. The Environmental Protection Agency has recognized The Home Depot, Costco, Menards, Ace Hardware and Sams Club for their education efforts and their promoting of CFLs.

Even my local Ace Hardware store owned by entrepreneur Bill Snyder adopted the merchandizing of sustainability as a competitive path against a new big box store built in our small town. Bill educates his customers with displays and in-store demos on the value and values of making their homes' green through a myriad of products. Two of his best selling products are a line of organic gardening products and a line of organic home cleaning products.

What the web-based green retailers never planned for, and to date have yet to achieve, is price leadership compared to the "Bill Snyders" who have cemented, branded relationships with the customer. In effect, the competitive path of least resistance was for existing retailers to change rather the strategic expectation held for green internet retailers that consumers would change from their traditional paths for making retail purchase.

That is the danger of beginning a strategy for selling green by initially focusing upon values. I hold the web green retailers I know in the highest regard. They know sustainability. Their ethics are admirable. I trust many of their sites because they are guardians against green washing. *But they have yet to demonstrate a compelling price advantage* and this is limiting their ability to grow to levels that would, like in First Solar's case, allow them to achieve economies of scale that enables a continuous improvement in their per unit price competitiveness. They failed to design a strategy like Give Something Back which understood from company's inception that they had to be competitive on price to win a bid.

In summary, a Crossing the Green Pricing Chasm™ strategy is a foundational key to accelerating and sustaining the growth of green revenues. Not being price competitive is at best a niche market strategy and it could be a path to business failure.

The first step in building a Crossing the Green Pricing Chasm™ strategy is identifying the target price goal like First Solar and Apple. The first *__implementation__* step in a Crossing the Pricing Chasm™ strategy is finding and selling early-adopter customers who will pay more for going green (in First Solar's case it was early-adopters in Europe and California) to create a pricing beach head. But the goal is to build from the beach head toward a mass marketing competitive advantage. A Crossing the Green Pricing Chasm™ strategy only works if you also have a path for growing the beach head into a mass movement for gaining price competitiveness compared to 20th Century legacy solutions and against competing sustainable businesses.

The huge advantage sustainable marketing has is a significantly sized group of beach head customers. Millennials are an obvious focus because they are the most likely of the Awareness Customers™ to pay more for going green because it means so much to their future. That is where Apple started with the iPod and iTunes. But in the Apple example, what they did brilliantly was to bring iTunes to the mass market by driving down the prices for iPods and establishing a compelling price per song. That is the same goal and process for building green revenues. Establish the beach head and drive to mass marketing with a compelling price.

The following graphic representation on the proportional weight I assign to creating a Crossing the Pricing Chasm™ will not sit well with those who I truly admire in the sustainability movement that are motivated by "doing right." But the reality of business is that price is where consumers begin in their procurement decision making process. There are a vast range of sustainable solutions but a major reason their mass adoption is not taking place is because these solutions are not "price competitive" to the mass market of consumers. The goal of this extreme pie-chart example is to shock you into thinking first about price competitiveness in the development of a business strategy for growing a sustainable business selling green.

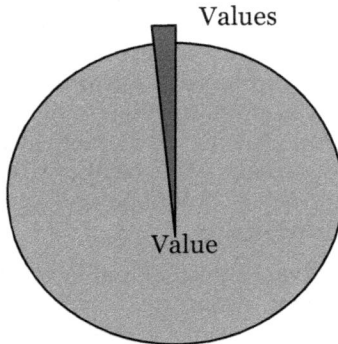

Values

Value

Is this too extreme of an example? Possibly. But the facts supporting this position are compelling. It was $5 per gallon gasoline that truly got Americans to again focus upon their gasoline consumption and the gas mileage of their cars. The car companies and energy companies that can come up with a sustainable, environmentally responsible answer that can beat the price-pants off of gasoline will harvest explosive revenue growth.

The fact the iPod was cool engaged the Millennials. But it was the ability to customize your music library at only 99 cents per song that made the iPod a mass market success. It isn't solely because the food is fresher at a farmer's market that this retail venue is exploding in its availability across America's cities. A major reason for the growth in farmer's markets is that they offer competitive prices compared to the grocery store.

Craigslist has a high degree of convenience, is green because it is digital rather than paper based, but the fact you can post an ad for free is its underlying competitive advantage compared to advertising in the newspaper. In summary, the facts are compelling that for a business to grow beyond a niche market it must offer sustainable solutions at a competitive price.

One of the key values I bring to my client's strategy analysis is helping them surface and answer these three questions:

1. "At what price will your product be the least cost, more meaning solution being sought by the Awareness Customer™?"

2. "What is your plan for gaining a price beach head with early adopter customers?

3. "What does it take to move your price from the beach head to the mass market?

From my experience it is the companies with a clear understanding on how to answer these questions that are experiencing high revenue growth and increased market share from selling green. Aligning Value to Values is the first ingredient in "The Secret Green Sauce™"!

And implementing your Crossing the Green Pricing Chasm™ strategy is the first step for making secret green sauce!

"The Secret Green Sauce"

Chapter Four

Branding
Prove It, Conclusively!™

Two key barriers confront all companies attempting to sell green by influencing consumer buying-behaviors. They are:

1. The consumer's current comfort zone of habit

2. Consumer's decision-making uncertainty tied to the massive misinformation being pumped out through greenwashing

The products that are experiencing rapid revenue growth and the companies that are winning market share are also the ones doing a great job of proving:

•   It really works

•   It is really sustainable

Green Works is the classic example of how to successfully grow a green consumer product to a large sales volume. And a key element of their strategy is "Prove It, Conclusively!™"

Green Works is a home cleaning product developed by the Clorox Corporation. The introduction of this product faced the following barriers to consumer adoption:

1. The parent company, Clorox, has manufacturing facilities and products with significantly sized emission footprints. The most likely early-adopter

customer for the product is Concerned Caregivers who could have a skeptical viewpoint of a cleaning product supplied by the manufacturer of bleach.

2. The target market of household cleaner buyers have strong loyalties to the cleaning products they use that go back to grandmothers telling their daughters who have told their daughters what type of household cleaner to use and why it is the best for their families. The idea of trying a new product *can feel* to these women like a breach in the family's lineage of knowledge, sharing and yes, even love.

3. Strong uncertainty and questioning among consumers on whether a "green" cleaning product could perform as well as a "strong chemical cleaning agent."

At the same time Clorox's marketing research found the basis for a Crossing the Chasm beach head strategy. The elements of their "Secret Green Sauce™" included:

1. There was a niche, but significantly sized, group of consumers seeking a "green" cleaning product that really was equal in its cleaning-performance to "non-green" cleaning products.

2. Price was important. The existing competition in green cleaning products, though developing strong reputations among early adopters for having a product that was an effective cleaner, typically cost significantly more than "non-green" cleaners.

3. Consumers wanted the convenience of buying a green cleaner from their traditional retailers. Many of the competing green cleaners were either sold via the web through a specialty site or at a smaller retail store that could be a further driving distance from the customer's home than the customer's normal shopping locations.

4. Clorox's identity among consumers as a manufacturer of bleach was actually a positive in terms of the company's credibility for supplying cleaning products that work.

"The Secret Green Sauce™" that Clorox produced has these core strategy features:

1. *The product is green.* The product consists of 99% natural ingredients including coconut and lemon oil. It is formulated to be biodegradable. It is non-allergenic. Its packaging is recyclable. And the product was not tested on animals.

2. *The product works.* In blind tests with consumers (a blind test means the consumers testing various products can't tell what product they are using) Green Works achieved performance parity with such major brands as Lysol, 409, and Pine-Sol. That was a hugely important achievement. It meant that if they could get consumers to try the product the consumers would find that it worked as well as their current, "non-green," cleaning products.

3. *It is sold through the big box retailers.* Clorox has strong business relationships with all the big box retailers. And one of their strongest relationships is with Walmart who has embraced sustainability as a path for growing revenues. Green Works' product introduction was perfectly timed with Walmart's search for green products to mass market. With Walmart's adoption of Green Works the other big boxes also began stocking the product.

4. *It is branded as a Clorox product.* Being a manufacturer of a bleach, while working against Clorox's image with environmentalists, worked for

Clorox in terms of credibility with consumers on the cleaning effectiveness of their cleaning products.

5. *It is lower in price compared to most other green cleaners and it is price competitive with many "non-green" cleaners.* Clorox is all about economies of scale and mass production to achieve price leadership. It is one of their significant competitive advantages. They used this competitive advantage to price Green Works dramatically lower than the existing green cleaning product competition and only marginally higher than "non-green" cleaning products. Clorox successfully implemented ""cost less, mean more"" by offering a highly competitive price that appeals to the mass market.

Even with this strategy there was resistance by consumers to trying a Clorox-produced green product because of the general "noise" of greenwashing being produced by legacy 20th Century companies. Clorox had to do more to prove their product, <u>conclusively</u>. On January 14, 2008 they announced that the Sierra Club had joined Clorox in promoting Green Works by allowing the Sierra Club logo to be placed on every bottle.

I will always remember this announcement. It was like feeling the green earth move under my feet. The Sierra Club really got blasted by some environmentalists. But the Sierra Club held to its position with reasoned evidence on why they thought Green Works was green. It appeared that the criticism may have actually backfired for the criticizing environmentalists. The media's coverage of the criticism increased the general public's awareness and increased understanding of Green Works's sustainable features based upon the highly credible manner with which the Sierra Club addressed the issue.

But Clorox really understands how to sell green. They knew that even gaining the Sierra Club's marketing participation that they, as all green companies do, face a need to achieve the result of "Prove it, conclusively™!"

Take a look at the Green Works bottle and their website. Green Works has these six "partners:"
1. Sierra Club
2. Good Housekeeping
3. US EPA's DfE Program
4. Clothing Swap, Inc
5. BlogHer
6. Rebuilding Greensburg Greener.

These SIX "partners" touch all the buttons-of-credibility a green cleaning product could ever envision:

- The world's leading environmental non-profit organization

- Good Housekeeping

- The Environmental Protection Agency

- A "green glamour" clothing website

- A women's blogging site focused upon the courageous efforts by a town destroyed by tornados that is rebuilding itself as a sustainable city.

Green Works is *"Proving It, Conclusively™!"*

What were the business results from Clorox deploying "Prove It, Conclusively™" as part of their "Secret Green Sauce™?" They were voted the number one U.S. Image Power Green Brand in WPP's 2009 Green Brands Global Survey (WPP is a global communications company with such leading marketing and PR companies as Burson-Marsteller, Cohn and Wolfe, Hill & Knowlton and Ogilvy & Mather Worldwide).

However commendable a prestigious public recognition is, the Clorox Corporation is run by a highly professional team of business leaders with a strong sense for the bottom line tied to goals for increasing stockholder value. And they have achieved a bottom line result of building Green Work's into a $100 million per year annual revenue product line. Green Works is one of the consumer product leaders in selling green.

The lessons learned are compelling for every green business and entrepreneur seeking to grow revenues selling green:

1. *A green revenue growth strategy must be focused upon the barriers to "closing a sale."* Price is hugely important. But so are legacy buying behaviors like family tradition, convenience and the consumer's tolerance for taking a procurement risk.

2. *Greenwashing is a major issue facing every green product and company.* Most companies will not be able to overcome consumer confusion and uncertainty just through advertising and branding. One very significant path for overcoming consumer confusion and uncertainty is to gain the endorsement of creditable third parties like a non-profit or from a group within the influence network that the targeted customers look to for advice and learning.

Certified coffees are a compelling example of the power associated with credible third party endorsements. The Rainforest Alliance has a program where they certify coffee grown to their standards based upon responsibility to the environment and to coffee field production workers (www.rainforest-alliance.org). Their certified coffees have an average growth in sales of 106 percent *each year* from 2003 through 2006. In 2007 over 91 million pounds of Rainforest Alliance Certified coffee was sold worldwide. In the U.S. these coffees are sold by Mars® Drinks, Wal-Mart, Whole Foods, Pom Wonderful and Caribou Coffee and can be found in more than 50,000 supermarkets, convenience stores, cafes, restaurants, hotels and corporate offices worldwide. Now that is what I am talking about in terms of the power of third party alliances to generate revenue growth!

3. *Prove It, Conclusively!*™ *is a core element in a green revenue growth strategy.* My own market research continues to document that an overwhelming majority of consumers are thirsting for labels that supply information meaningful to their product evaluation process, that are simple to read and that "scream" credibility. Failing to achieve Prove it, Conclusively™ will limit a green revenue growth strategy to a niche market of early-adopter customers who are willing to do the leg-work of figuring out if a product has appealing and credible benefits. Don't put your customers into the position of trying to figure it out. Prove it to them, conclusively!

Chapter Five

Marketing
"Know It, Embrace It"

A question I am continuously asked by companies seeking to grow green revenues is:

"How do you sell to green customers?"

That is actually a very insightful question. **The old system of advertising is NOT the path being used by the Awareness Customer™ to figure out what to buy and what companies they want to buy from.**

The Awareness Customer™ is moving past the traditional advertising model of sound bites sandwiched between radio and TV programming as something they use to make green purchase decisions. Two "negative-drivers" for why Awareness Customers™ are looking beyond traditional media advertising in terms of their sustainability procurement decisions are:

- Greenwashing by companies making green claims that are not aligned with the Awareness Customer's definition of green

- The ongoing erosion of leadership credibility as our country endures more business scandals and bankruptcies.

Rather than relying upon advertising_the Awareness Customer™ is engaged in an interactive process of:

- Searching

- Interconnecting

- Learning

- Implementing changes in their buying behavior

- *Reporting their experience.*

The Awareness Customer™ searches a myriad of internet sites like Good Guide, Consumer Reports and Planet Green that provide an array of professional technical assessments, experiential feedback from consumers and computer generated price comparisons between competing suppliers and products. And they use Internet interconnectivity (Web 2.0: blogs, Facebook, Twitter, etc.) to explore stakeholder-outreach paths that increase their awareness on products, companies, issues and people. Tellingly, YouTube is now second only to Google in BUSINESS searches.

Most importantly, the Awareness Customer™ RESPONDS through Web 2.0 by offering their insights on what they have learned, how they are implementing sustainability and who was helpful to them (So many Concerned Caregivers are blogging they now have a label, "Mommy bloggers." One estimate from a green retailer is that there are now 20 million mommy bloggers!)

This interaction is creating the following *Awareness Customer Dynamic*™:

Sustainability 2.0

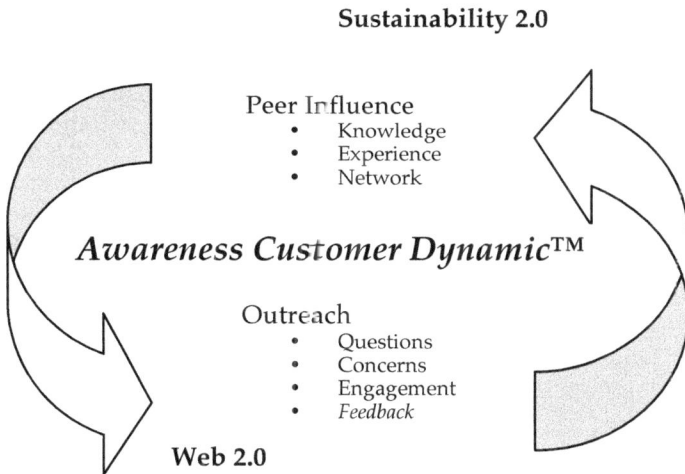

Peer Influence
- Knowledge
- Experience
- Network

Awareness Customer Dynamic™

Outreach
- Questions
- Concerns
- Engagement
- *Feedback*

Web 2.0

The Awareness Customer Dynamic™ *is a continuous loop of learning, doing and sharing.* It is a merger of the tools of Web 2.0 with what the Awareness Customer Network™ has now labeled Sustainability 2.0 (the process of implementing sustainable actions).

The University of San Diego has a webpage on Sustainability 2.0. They define Sustainability 2.0 as integrating "research, education and application." *An entrepreneur web-expert within my network has labeled this confluence of Web 2.0 and Sustainability 2.0 as* **"Know It, Embrace It.***"*

Am I being an extremist to suggest this is an awareness revolution? Insert this link into your web-browser:

http://walmartstores.com/Sustainability/8844.aspx.

There you will find Walmart's video entitled Sustainability 2.0. There is also a companion video entitled "Sustainability 2.0-Goals" that is an outline of Walmart's goals for aligning with the Awareness Customer™. I recently heard a professional economist estimate that one out of every three dollars spent in the world is "touched" directly by Walmart or indirectly through one of their supply-chain partners. I cannot image a stronger signal for every business, entrepreneur and investor that a new day is dawning for growing green revenues and green market share than Walmart's commitment to Sustainability 2.0.

The path for growing green revenues *goes through* the Awareness Customer's™ reliance upon interconnectivity with their Awareness Customer Networks™. This interconnectivity is enabling the Awareness Customer™ to be continuously engaged in a self-learning implementation process on how to consume sustainably (answering every imaginable question from what are bio-fuels, where to find a green job, why Global Warming is real, how to install a low flow water faucet, when to plant organic tomatoes, etc., etc.). And the success of one Awareness Customer™ in figuring out a "green answer" migrates as educational-information that <u>encourages</u> change within the Awareness Customer Networks™.

The keys to selling green are:

1. **Being an educational-information** resource within the Awareness Customer's™ Web 2.0 *interconnectivity process* and,

2. *A solution* within their Sustainability 2.0 *implementation process.*

Implementing these keys to selling green by adding value to the Awareness Customer Dynamic™ consists of the three steps identified by the University of San Diego:

1. Research.
   Selling to the Awareness Customer™ doesn't begin with a sales pitch but rather a question or an issue. And typically the best questions are being raised by the Awareness Customer™. The companies that are being successful growing green revenues are doing a strong job of stakeholder outreach that begins with listening to the Awareness Customers'™ questions and concerns.

2. Education.
   The typical advertising model sees "Education" as what they want to achieve with the customer, as in, the company educating the customer. It is my experience that companies successfully growing green revenues view education as something that occurs within their business across the broadest range of work associates achieved by linking to their Awareness Customer's™ *self-educating* process. These companies are participating in the Awareness Customer Networks™. And they harvest value by converting this learning into sales by selling goods and services that meet the Awareness Customer's search for less cost, more meaning. Clorox didn't launch Green Works with the Sierra Club's marketing participation but they listened to the Awareness

Customer's search for credibility and developed a revenue growing solution. Give Something Back didn't begin their business selling green products. Their superior ability at listening to their customers (and work associates) pulled them into selling sustainable solutions. Apple really doesn't see itself as "green" but rather as cool. But they are green because the products their customers wanted also turned out to be a sustainable alternative to buying music embedded on plastic disks that came packaged in throw-away paper and plastic, all of which was purchased by driving a car to an air-conditioned or heated retail store.

Where I see companies continuously fail is when their legacy systems impede their ability to learn/align with the Awareness Customer's™ self-educational process. Ironically, the legacy companies and their traditional metrics are greenwashing themselves. How many ads do we now see from 20th Century companies talking about how they are going green and yet their green efforts pale in size and strategic significance to their "unsustainable" business systems? Do they really think their ads are engaging the Awareness Customer™? In too many cases they are talking to themselves and spending big money doing so. Such efforts may produce lobbying benefits but not sustainable alignment with Awareness Customers™ that are seeking companies that provide "cost less, mean more" goods and services.

3. Application.
   This is where companies like Apple, Walmart and Clorox are pioneering how to realize green sales success through aligning with the Awareness Customer™. Apple owns cool and their creativity has created a sustainable system for listening to music, and soon, watching videos. The Millennials love them

and their moms, The Concerned Caregivers, are climbing aboard by buying iPhones. Clorox is "inside the heads" of Concerned Caregivers. Their Green Works product achieved $100 million of annual revenues by hitting all the buttons of concerns and expectations held by Concerned Caregivers who see sustainability as a path for enhancing the wellness of their loved ones. In addition, Clorox heard the CEO of Walmart loud and clear on his strategic decision that Walmart would be a leading green merchant. Clorox now supplies Walmart with a green product that is growing green revenues for Walmart. By adopting Sustainability 2.0 in their businesses, their business strategies and product designs these green business leaders are learning by doing with growing green revenues as the performance result gained from this interactive process.

And often the path of engagement with the Awareness Customer™ (most especially the Millennials and Concerned Caregivers) is through Web 2.0. *It is a digital referral system.* It is a thousand forums where the Awareness Customers™ goes to:

- Gain knowledge

- Share knowledge

- Collaborate on projects/learning

- Socially network

- Gain transparency on who is saying what for what reasons

- Diversify their access to information, people and businesses

Like any experiential customer referral system Web 2.0 is brutally honest. The powerful are not powerful unless their information and integrity supports a position of credibility. It is a community of diversity linked by common interests or concerns. *It is the path for green businesses and entrepreneurs to find and win customers based upon their ability to align value with values.*

Web 2.0 is how I learn. For example, I was interviewing an engineering professional regarding a prospective advisory board member role for a client company when he mentioned he was a national expert on organic tomato sauce. After the interview I went to my computer and searched "organic tomatoes." You can find networks of people talking about how to grow them. You can find networks of people sharing their favorite tomato sauce recipes. You can find issue-discussions on why "grocery store" tomatoes are not sustainable and data on the carbon footprint of a "hot house tomato" defined by distance traveled to market, use of chemical fertilizers, etc. And yes, my interview candidate was an expert on organic tomato sauce. Today there isn't a sustainability topic that is without a Web 2.0 forum for sharing issue-data and for discussing what is working and who is doing what. Web 2.0 is an unbelievable door into understanding what the Awareness Customer™ wants to buy and who they what to buy from.

Systems Thinking Tools

So the next question is:

*"How does a company use Web 2.0,
the Awareness Customer Dynamic™
and Sustainability 2.0 to create a strategy
for growing green revenues?"*

A key tool I use in developing "outside the box" strategies is called Systems Thinking. I had the opportunity to study under Dr. Peter Senge, the author of the Fifth Discipline and a leader in Systems Thinking. Peter is a MIT professor who, along with Professor Jay Forrester, developed tools for capturing the causal impacts of influence drivers impacting a system, like a business. I have found Systems Thinking to be a hugely important tool in figuring out sustainability strategies because the key influence-drivers upon this strategy design process are typically outside the "norm".

In economics these outside-the-norm influence-drivers are called "externalities." Chapter One, The Collapse of "Unsustainability", listed some of the key environmental and social externalities that are influencing a revolution in how businesses do business. And Chapter Two, The Awareness Customer™, profiled the emergence of a new class of consumer that can be an "externality" to 20th Century companies focused upon their traditional marketing metrics. I use Systems Thinking to enable a company to quantify the "curve of change" created by externalities (rarely is change linear, it is most often a curve of initially-slower change that can accelerate as technologies, *competitors* and new customers emerge).

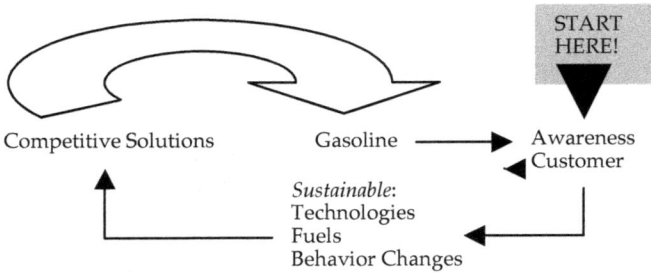

For example, ten years from now selling gasoline is not going be the same business as it is today. For one thing it will be a lot more expensive per gallon. The causes for this price increase are externalities. The price at the pump isn't going up because the oil companies are operating less efficiently or because they are using market power to artificially raise prices. The price is going up because the world demand for oil is increasing faster than supply, because the world's financial market is now using oil as a hedge to manage the currency risks of the U.S. dollar and because world governments are beginning to tax emissions. The combination of the strong world demand for oil (even in the face of a global recession), the U.S. government printing trillions of dollars and the introduction of new taxes upon emissions will continue the upward price spiral at the pump.

Another externality is the Awareness Customers'™ response to increasing gasoline prices and Global Warming (another externality). Examples of this response include corporate-fleets reducing their carbon footprint in response to their CEO's CO_2 emission reduction mandates and in so doing exploring alternative technologies, fuels and energy efficiency paths. Concerned Caregivers are questioning their love of large SUVs and many are experimenting with buying hybrids. And the Millennials are really experimenting with everything from moving into a more densely urban lifestyle that is less reliant upon gasoline powered cars ("Eco-cities, living together, driving less") to working at home rather than commuting.

In response to this evidence of new business opportunities there has been an explosion in the number of green businesses and entrepreneurs proposing new ideas for sustainable fuels and cars. This competitive challenge is yet another "externality."

Systems Thinking is a tool for capturing the cause and effect dynamics of externalities upon a business system like those outlined in the "gasoline" example. The goal of using Systems Thinking tools is not to predict future events or attempt to pinpoint the date of "change." Rather, Systems Thinking is a tool that enables dialogue and learning on what is influencing change and how various "externality-scenarios" could impact business performance. The use of Systems Thinking enables a business to quantify the "curve of change" and link future change scenarios to their performance metrics. The result is that participants in the Systems Thinking process self-develop "stories" that capture the essence of a key change dynamic like the "Boiling Frog" that tells how an organization could decline through incremental externality impacts that in their singular go unnoticed (or more accurately, under-appreciated) but in their accumulation generate severe damage. (The name Boiling Frog comes from the example where if a frog is dropped into a pot of boiling water it will jump out but if the frog is placed in a pot of room temperature water that is slowly brought to a boil the frog stays in the pot and dies.) Stories like the Boiling Frog facilitate internal communication of complex concepts and they enable consensus around a vision of how their business should respond to change.

Systems Thinking is an excellent tool for "cutting across" a business built around organizational silos of Finance, Marketing, Manufacturing, Customer Service, R&D, etc. A silo organizational design can experience challenges developing a green strategic plan that aligns value with values to win sales from the Awareness Customer™ as each silo touches their part of the "elephant" without achieving the necessary enterprise-scale perspective that realizes how big the elephant is and most importantly, where the elephant is heading. Systems Thinking provides tools for engaging with all stakeholders to surface their "curve of change" vision, for exercising "curve of change" scenarios as a collaborative learning process and most importantly, to surface *enterprise-scale* paths for aligning value with values to win sales from Awareness Customers™.

One great example is a large law firm that self-engaged in a Systems Thinking-like approach toward going green. Imagine a law firm that isn't based upon paper. That was the enterprise-scale future that surfaced from their visioning process. Their performance-vision for moving to a digital system included dramatically lower operating costs and increased efficiency as lawyers gained superior portability and access to digital data that their current paper files in a central storage location could never achieve. The process took two years of much internal "angst" as historical behaviors had to be overcome. The dramatic result was this law firm's COO standing before a conference of CFOs holding in one hand the very small silver metal trashcan that represented the waste basket each lawyer now uses! Its size was barely large enough to hold a six pack of Coca Cola. The financial result of this transformation was lower operating costs, a lower carbon footprint, increased human-resources productivity and an enhanced market positioning as a green law firm. Home Run!

Another example I like is the Ritz-Carlton, Kapalua on Maui, Hawaii. This case study is an example of what is called "An Unintended Consequence" in System Thinking. It is a story I see often among green businesses where one effort at marketing sustainability often grows additional revenue opportunities. In the case of the Ritz-Carlton, Kapalua they started a marketing program for the children of guests called the Jean-Michel Cousteau's Ambassadors of the Environment. But the kids came back with such great experiences that their parents began to ask if they could participate. As awareness increased that environmental education was attractive to guests the idea surfaced to plant a garden with native food plants on the hotel grounds. The hotel's chef began to harvest the vegetables and fruits to enhance the in-hotel dining experience. The end result is that this new native foods menu has increased the hotel's food service revenues! System Thinking is a great vehicle for exploring for these types of "Unintended Consequences" revenue opportunities.

Unfortunately, a Hudson Gain Corporation study documents the distance Corporate America still needs to travel to achieve results comparable to the case studies of the green law firm or the Ritz-Carlton, Kapalua. The Hudson Gain study identified "Cost Savings" as the primary focus of Corporate America for going green. Corporate America's key metric was the Finance Department's Return on Equity. My personal anecdotes of working with Corporate America is littered with great sustainable projects that never saw the light of day because they did not achieve the CFO's two-year cash flow re-payment criterion for making a "non-strategic" capital investment. Most importantly, and the theme of this book, a cost focus for going green misses the real business opportunity. A business cannot be sustained only on cost cutting. It requires revenues and ideally, revenue growth. **That is the opportunity of the Green Economic Revolution for business, namely, a path for growing revenues.**

The other key areas identified in this study as drivers identified by Corporate America as reasons for going green were avoidance of legal risk and some potential, but hard to quantify, enhancement in their brand equity. The focus upon risk avoidance is the legal-department's silo effort at bringing to management's attention that there is a growing government focus upon emissions and that prudence would dictate deploying measurement tools to identify a corporation's potential for litigation or negative regulatory actions. The marketing departments in many corporations do see the same market research I see and understand that a marketing sea-change is occurring. But because their influence to effect organizational change competes with other silos within the organization their efforts are often limited to exploring paths for placing "green" on their brands and in their marketing campaigns.

One of my most frustrating experiences in being a Green Business Coach mirrors exactly the findings of the Hudson Gain Corporation. I was engaged by a marketing VP for a major telecommunications company because the key-account clients of this company were beginning to introduce sustainability into their bid procurement criteria. Protocol required that he place me in contact with the individual responsible for buying energy. This energy buyer actually "got it" and a business concept emerged for building a roof-top solar power plant at a headquarters building with the intent that it would be a marketing vehicle that could be used in aligning with not only the growing number of key-accounts adding sustainable bid criteria but also as a marketing path toward Millennials and Concerned Caregivers, both of which were significant retail customers for this company's products.

The tragedy of the opportunity began as various corporate silos came together into a committee. The purchasing department took control of the process and created a bidding-system for selecting a solar panel supplier based upon price/features optimization (logical for buying a commodity like energy but not aligned with the need for engaging the Awareness Customer™). The building operations and maintenance department began specifying installation criteria that narrowed the opportunity to demonstrate technology leadership. The CFO's department insisted upon financial paybacks traditionally applied to "non-strategic" investments like an onsite power plant and by doing so eliminate all but a handful of potential suppliers who had the capacity of financing the project off balance sheet.

The entire process lost the initial direction of creating a breakthrough marketing opportunity to increase sales by aligning with their growing numbers of Awareness Customers™. The committee reported success back to management based upon achieving their performance metrics for a least cost solar power plant, installed in the manner preferred by the building maintenance department while the marketing department gained a press release that went unnoticed by the Awareness Customer™. Where this company lost an opportunity was in maintaining its focus upon aligning their product offerings with their Awareness Customers™. Their committee decision making system shifted their internal focus upon communicating their own performance results to themselves. The result was a "successful" project that did nothing to align with their Awareness Customers™.

Even in those companies focused upon increasing their sustainability commitment through green team deployments the organization of green teams are often by department-silo. Some green teams do use sophisticated analysis tools like Systems Thinking. Most typically use brainstorming tools to identify ideas within their silo, they use experimentation to search for opportunities that align with corporate performance-metric goals and they generate good projects that achieve incremental change to their existing systems. Often the efforts to engage outside stakeholders are limited to setting goals for their supply chain partners to lower costs and emissions.

The opportunity potentially being missed is for using tools like Systems Thinking to surface the essence of the Green Economic Revolution within a corporation's green team process that are often structured around the company's organizational silos and constrained by a near-term focus. Most especially, a potential missed opportunity is to enhance learning on the emerging Awareness Customer™ though "Know It, Embrace It" engagement paths. For example, Give Something Back's business model for selling green is focused upon figuring out ideas for making their customers more sustainable at competitive prices. See the difference compared to the survey of Corporate America and their focus upon cost reduction, legal risk mitigation and a vague path toward brand equity improvement? Give Something Back's core business strategy is built around responsibility toward the environment, society, their associates and most especially, their customers. Their company's *external focus* is one big organizational Systems Thinking strategy in action that is achieving superior market share and revenue growth results.

"Know It, Embrace It" For Selling Green

"Know It, Embrace It" is the mantra for selling green because The Awareness Customer™ is focused upon externalities. These customers are looking past legacy systems toward living and working in a sustainable way that will provide them with lower costs while addressing their environmental/societal/wellness concerns.

The winning green companies and products have this same focus. They understand what is relevant to all stakeholders and identify price competitive solutions. They don't "advertise." Rather they build bridges that enable the Awareness Customer™ to shape their business strategies and product designs. The inputs into their strategic thinking come from learning what the Awareness Customer™ is saying on Web 2.0 and what the Awareness Customer™ is implementing through Sustainability 2.0. The winning green companies growing green revenues "Know It, Embrace It!"

Chapter Six

Human Resources Plan
Green Jobs/Green Teams

To build a successful green revenue growth strategy a company will need work associates who can enable a strategic path for selling "less cost, mean more" products and services to the Awareness Customers™.

I participate as a volunteer in educational programs typically organized by churches to help those in job transition. A key message I deliver to this audience is that all businesses will need green work associates and every profession will someday be "green." I ask them to imagine trying to be CPA, or auto mechanic or CEO without knowing how to operate a computer? I explain that this is where we are heading in terms of the Green Economic Revolution. Every work associate will be expected to know how their tasks impact the Awareness Customer's™ pursuit of less cost, more meaning.

The ramifications for human resources management are obviously dramatic. It impacts who an organization should be hiring. It impacts who an organization should be promoting. It has huge impacts upon job training similar to the introduction of the PC where everyone in the organization will need ongoing education and information as what is "green" grows and changes as sustainability accelerates its integration into the company's business systems.

As previously mentioned, green teams are a great vehicle for realizing work associate training and organizational change (especially when, as discussed in Chapter Five, "Know It, Embrace It," the green teams are enabled with Systems Thinking tools). Green teams are aligned with the Awareness Customer's™ learning methodology of achieving through engagement. Successful green teams engage the work associate by asking them to:

- Research reasons for change

- Brainstorm for meaningful change

- Experiment with achieving measurable results

- Share their knowledge through outreach with their fellow associates.

Green teams are springing up across Corporate America. One of many examples is an international gaming and hotel chain with over 30 green teams that are working on over 130 projects. They can point to an impressive list of accomplishments that have saved millions of dollars and that have reduced their carbon footprint (and their water and waste-stream footprints). And their competitors are forming green teams too. There are few industries in Corporate America where I could not point to at least one company that has formed green teams which are realizing cost saving results.

Eight Keys to Green Team Success

The best green teams have these characteristics:

1. Volunteers.
   Often the first green teams consist of volunteers who are motivated to make a difference through sustainability. A volunteer is the ideal member for

a green team. And what is really cool is that as green teams produce results their members "brag" and that draws increased interest in others who would like to achieve similar results. Green team volunteers are like internal-Awareness Customers™ leading a movement toward less cost, more meaning.

2. Start With "Low-Hanging Fruit."
    Yes, many participants in green teams are highly motivated to achieve change and sometimes this can result in a team biting off more than they can chew. The reality is that in most companies the steps toward change need to begin incrementally. A key first step for green teams is to prove that change is beneficial. For this reason in many companies, the first effort of a green teams should be low-key and it should target a sure win. This is the "get to first base" strategy that always works in terms of building credibility within a company and with management.

3. Executive Sponsors.
    Start with one if you can, win one you must. A "best practice" for green teams is to have the team initially focus upon improving a business performance metric that is important to a senior leader. Walking into a senior leader's office with a plan for, and then actually achieving, an improvement in how that senior leader measures performance (which typically ties to their bonus and promotion potential) is the surest way to gain an executive sponsor.

4. Brainstorm, Focus, Then Execute.
    Many successful green teams begin by deploying a tactical process of brainstorming for ideas, then going through a group consensus process for

aligning their focus and then developing action items for achieving results. This is a tried and proven path for incremental progress. As the concept of green teams gains traction the enterprise's senior leadership will need to arm their green teams with strategic direction and Systems Thinking-like tools or expect the process of picking-off lowering hanging fruit to reach its natural result of diminishing returns.

5.   Retain Experts.
The reality of "going green" is that often this can be new territory for green team members. It may also be a case where outside knowledge and experience is needed on technical issues not housed within the green teams' membership. Retaining experts who understand the process and have technical expertise that the group might not have among its membership can produce faster and more meaningful results.

6.   Engage your supply chain.
This is a national trend. It is highly likely one or more of your supply partners are using green teams too. Plug in with them on what is working. Find out if they have resources to help make your green team's successful. Set common goals. Believe me, your best suppliers will love that you are asking and will leap to respond.

7.   Celebrate Success.
Success breeds success. One of my favorite forms of celebration is a green drinks or cook-out event after work (there is, in-fact, an organization that holds Green Drinks where people with an interest in sustainability can network during happy hour: www.greendrinks.org). If an after-hours event is too outside the box then explore hosting a green

breakfast, or lunch or just a meeting. But the purpose is to create enthusiasm and engage potential new green team members. One green team I know of brings in fresh fruits and vegetables grown in their own gardens that they invite their fellow work associates to pick up at the green team member's desks. You can imagine the sharing that takes place as a non-green work associate picks up a piece of fresh fruit at a green team member's desk!

8. Engage Senior Management.
    At some point good green teams need financial and authorization support. This is usually achieved as a process. Invite management to your celebrations. Brief management in person or via memo on your team's goals, plans and achievements. Surface resource requirements within the normal budgeting process. Do surveys of fellow work associates, your suppliers, or competitors. And best of all, survey your customers. Providing management with ongoing testimonials from customers on why going green is important to them will help them see the potential that aligning value with values has for increasing sales and brand loyalty.

Visit www.sustainablesiliconvalley.org to find more ideas from actual green teams.

There are two elements that are implicit in building a human resources plan that supports the introduction of sustainability as a core business strategy. One is senior management's support. Today CEOs are members of Awareness Customers™ based upon their goal to reduce CO_2 emissions. The result is an organizational focus upon internal operations that impact the carbon footprint. This is wonderful in terms of an environmental goal but the major premise of this book is that a sea-changing business opportunity is emerging through a global Green Economic Revolution. And every company I know of that is growing green revenues has senior management endorsement for a strategy that looks beyond reductions in an organization's carbon footprint.

The other key element is the development of an enterprise scale strategy for growing green. Apple didn't develop iTunes as a path for lowering internal operating costs. It was a path toward achieving revenue growth. Caribou is not selling Rainforest Alliance certified coffees because this product is less expensive than non-certified coffees. They are selling Rainforest Alliance certified coffees because their customers are buying this product in such volumes that they are experiencing double and triple digit sales volume increases. Give Something Back didn't plan to "go green." They have a strategy built upon responsibility. But their CUSTOMERS (and work associates) "pulled" them into going green and now they are growing revenues selling sustainable products and services.

For a company's human resources department to realize their potential role in helping their company grown green revenues they will need senior management to establish this as a strategic goal. One proactive role that the human resources departments can fulfill because their activities do cut across the organizational silos is to design special learning events that surface outside the box discussions. This is very Web 2.0 in style by inviting management to participate in topic discussions that are facilitated with data, experts and case-study insights on how other companies are building green revenue growth strategies. The goal is engagement. The process is participation. The result would ideally be enhanced awareness. The product would be ongoing dialogue. The impact could be measurable change in seeking paths for going (and ideally selling) green.

And when a company does integrate sustainability at the core of its business strategy then the HR department will need to enable the existing work associates with training programs to equip them with the knowledge and tools to implement sustainability.

Tied to this role of training is another hugely important role the HR Department could play. It involves the concept of the "green-entrepreneurship." Companies that have pioneered implementing sustainability often have done so through their own green-entrepreneurs who have the vision, knowledge and skills to create business performance results on a business-unit scale.

HR has a key role in identifying green-entrepreneurs candidates, in helping a company develop green-entrepreneurs and in recruiting green-entrepreneurs. This is a tremendous opportunity for the human resources department to provide strategic empowerment to their company by re-tooling, training and recruiting the people the enterprise must have to achieve green sales success.

Finally, there was an explosion within Corporate America about two years ago in the creation of a new senior officer, the Chief Sustainability Officer. In many companies these officers are enabling real change that is achieving reduction in their company's footprint and meaningful cost savings success. Some Chief Sustainability Officers have the power to execute change. Most have the ability to influence through their knowledge, interpersonal skills and officer title. Much of their focus has been in helping their companies understand the issues, develop diagnostic tools, gain adoption of performance goals and assist in the implementation process engineering, often through green teams. This effort also typically engages the company's supply chain partners who probably have also created Chief Sustainability Officers within their companies. The Chief Sustainability Officer in many companies have built such high levels of enterprise-scale credibility through realization of cost savings performance improvements that they are now positioned to explore expanding their focus through outreach with the sales and marketing departments and other potential strategic allies that are sensing the opportunity to increase sales by going green. Such a move from footprint and cost focus to sales and marketing is a naturally progressive path for Chief Sustainability Officers in their role as the awareness and enabling officer for realizing business opportunities through sustainability's adoption by the enterprise.

In summary, the successful companies selling green are doing so because they have developed human resources who "Know It, Embrace It." Many are using green teams as paths for incremental improvements in cost savings and footprint reductions. And Habitat Suites in Austin, Texas has the best human resources story I have hear to date where it has been eight years since they had their last turn over in their human resources. Management attributes two key reasons for this remarkable retention success. The first is the loyalty among work associates for the the hotel gained from giving associates surplus food from the onsite food garden. The second comes an appreciation of increased personal safety held by the associates from working in an environment free of toxic chemicals.

However, as green teams progress inside Corporate America, they will face a fork-in-the-road moment. They can continue to have a "reduction" focus on costs and emissions that will increasingly confront diminishing returns as the next incremental improvement becomes more expensive or difficult. The alternative is to begin the process of looking externally toward the growth in the Awareness Customers™ market segment to find new opportunities tied to increasing sales and growing market share. It will be through a company's human resources that the potential path for selling green will be executed. The successful companies are enabling their associates and empowering their HR departments to facilitate this process. Companies that do not will soon find themselves losing market share and sales to companies deploying *green* work associates.

As a HR professional maybe you are not convinced? Here's one last piece of food-for-thought. Guess who started Give Something Back's first green team? It was their HR Director!

Chapter Seven

Increasing Stock Valuation!
How to successfully engage the CFO

In drafting this book's outline I toyed with making this chapter the first chapter of the book. The reason is obvious. Every time I talk with investors and the senior management of companies I am asked this question:

"Is sustainability a path
for building stockholder value?"

Now I have the answer thanks to someone I hope will be as famous as Edward C. Johnson III, the founder of Fidelity Investments, the world largest mutual fund company. His name is R. Paul Herman. He is the founder of the HIP Investor, Inc.

Paul is one of those really bright guys who can use financial analysis to gain insights that have that "wow" factor. And what is wowing me is that he is generating evidence that companies that are more sustainable achieve higher stockholder valuation than companies that are less sustainable.

How much better? Paul explains,

"The HIP 100 approach has out-performed the S&P 100 benchmark ***by more than 400 basis*** points on average in recent time periods, in both up and down markets."

This quotes is in the largest type used within this book for a reason. 100 basis points is equivalent to a 1% return upon investment. So in an economy where the average long term interest rate of return on a 10 year U.S. Treasury note is currently less than 4% then the idea that companies that are more sustainable are earning 400 basis points higher returns on their stock valuations should gain the immediate attention of every CEO, CFO and equity investor in America!

So what is the basis of Paul's research claims? The HIP 100 Index is a re-weighting of the S&P 100 portfolio based upon Paul's statistical evaluation of an individual company's HIP ("human impact + profits"). ExxonMobil is a good example. Based upon its relative size compared to other companies, ExxonMobil represents approximately 4% of the S&P 100 Index portfolio. The HIP 100 Index has ExxonMobil weighted at approximately 1% because the company has an oil-industry leading carbon footprint that could significantly impact ExxonMobil's future earnings if Cap and Trade is adopted as a pricing model for carbon emissions.

Get it? *Paul is using* **_the economics of sustainability_** *in evaluating stockholder valuations.* And the results are that the HIP 100 Index is outperforming the S&P 100 Index in both up or down markets!

So what is HIP? Here's my take on how Paul conducts a statistical evaluation of a company based these factors:

1. Health.
    The health analysis quantifies answers to the question of "How does a company's products and initiatives improve the health, extend the life, or benefit the quality of life of customers, employees or suppliers?"

2. Wealth.
   The wealth analysis quantifies answers to the question of "How does a company's products and initiatives increase the income or assets (or reduce the debt or taxes) of customers, employees or suppliers?"

3. Earth.
   The earth analysis quantifies answers to the question of "What are the environmental impacts of a company's products and services, including a company's carbon footprint?"

4. Equality.
   The equality analysis quantifies answers to the question of "How representative is a company's leaders, work associates and suppliers compared to the demographic profile of their overall market segment and customers?

5. Trust.
   The trust analysis quantifies answers to the question of "To what degree does a company's decision-making-process look beyond the profit motive to include corporate responsibility, ethics and morality?"

Here is one interesting example related to Paul's research. Catalyst.org is a non-profit "working globally with businesses and the professions to build inclusive workplaces and expand opportunities for women and business. Catalyst.org's research has documented that the return on equity achieved by companies with *more* women on the board of directors compared to the returns achieved by companies with the least number of women board of directors was <u>up to 53% higher</u>! One reason for this stunning result is the reality that women do represent a little over 50% of the U.S. population and represent approximately $8.5 billion in annual buying power. So having women on the board of directors of a company should enhance a company's ability to provide leadership direction on selling to women.

But in terms of selling green the Catalyst.org research is also very interesting. One of the three Awareness Customer™ drivers is Concerned Caregivers, women! Having more women on a board of directors is a path for creating a business advantage in aligning a company's strategies with the Concern Caregiver's adoption of sustainability. What is so cool about Paul's research is that he is exploring exactly this type of analysis. And so should every company that wants to grow green revenues as a path for increasing stockholder value.

The research methodology conducted by Capital E is a great example for companies looking to find increased opportunity for their green team. (Capital E is a premier provider of strategic consulting, technology assessment and deployment and advisory services to firms and investors in the clean energy industry.) The typical analysis I am familiar with for commercial buildings is focused upon quantifying the financial payback opportunity achieved through cost reductions for energy (and increasingly, water). Capital E did evaluate the financial benefits of a green building based upon energy cost savings. Their analysis from energy savings documented about a $6 Net Present Value per sq. ft based upon investments that ranged between $3-5 per sq. ft. But when they expanded their analysis to include operational and maintenance savings and human productivity gains measured in terms of fewer days lost to illness and a higher level of productivity achieved by working in a people friendly environment they calculated a Net Present Valuation that ranged between $40-60 per sq. ft. for the $3-5 per sq. ft. investment. The implications are that companies looking beyond the traditional two year return upon investment criteria by incorporating "HIP-like" analysis are harvesting superior operating results that should translate into superior stock valuation results.

The University of San Diego's Burnham-Moores Center for Real Estate and CB Richard Ellis (CBRE) achieved similar results in a study they did on the performance impacts of people working in green buildings. Their criteria of performance were sick days and self-reported productivity. What their research found was that 45% of the associates working in Energy Star or LEED certified buildings had fewer sick days with only 10% reporting higher sick days. And 55% of the work associates reported a higher level of productivity with only 2% reporting lower productivity. This study calculated a $20+ value creation per 250 sq. ft of work associate space through lower absences due to illness and increased productivity based upon their survey results.

There is also emerging data tied to Merger & Acquisition results on the increasing stockholder valuation assigned to businesses that have successfully pioneered selling green. Here are just three examples:

- Clorox buying Burt's Bees, a leader in natural personal care products, for $900+ million.

- Coca-Cola buying Odwalla, a leader in organic beverages, for $181 million and Republic Tea, a leader in organic tea bags, for $43 million

- Colgate-Palmolive buying Tom's of Maine, a leader in natural toothpaste and other personal care products, for $100 million.

Phil Howard, Assistant Professor, Dept. of Community, Agriculture, Recreation and Resource Studies, Michigan State University has produced a really cool graphic showing how 20th Century consumer product companies have accelerated their offering of green products through acquisition. His chart shows Heinz's strategic alliance with Hain Celestial and their 21 organic brand acquisitions that include Celestial Seasonings and Spectrum Organics. And there is Kellogg which has bought Morningstar Farms/Natural Touch, Kashi, Wholesome & Hearty and Bear Naked. It is a strong stockholder valuation signal when companies with an "ear for the customer" like Coca-Cola, Kellogg and Colgate-Palmolive are buying or entering into strategic alliances with companies that have pioneered growing green revenues.

In summary, there is growing evidence that sustainability is a path for growing stockholder value. R. Paul Herman's research demonstrates that a focus upon human impact and profits can produce sustained and meaningful stockholder valuation performance. Analysis like that performed by Catalyst.org and Capital E are linking the data points between going green, selling green and making green. And the acquisitions by some of our world's most astute consumer products companies are pointing toward an exciting future for entrepreneurs who can grow the next generation of green enterprises that will valued by larger companies as acquisition paths for accelerating their market appeal to the Awareness Customer™.

Chapter Eight

Strategic Plan
The Secret Green Sauce Recipe™

This diagram is your recipe for creating your own "Secret Green Sauce™."

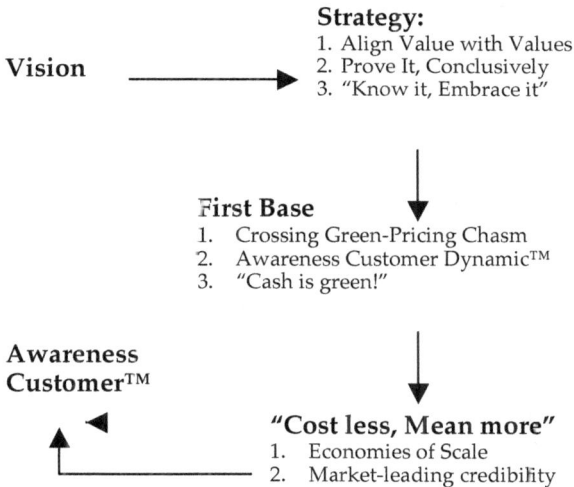

Vision ⟶

Strategy:
1. Align Value with Values
2. Prove It, Conclusively
3. "Know it, Embrace it"

↓

First Base
1. Crossing Green-Pricing Chasm
2. Awareness Customer Dynamic™
3. "Cash is green!"

↓

Awareness Customer™
◄

"Cost less, Mean more"
1. Economies of Scale
2. Market-leading credibility

And Amanda's is my favorite example of how to create a recipe for The Secret Green Sauce that will grow a profitable, significantly sized business.

Amanda's is a healthy fast food restaurant created by Amanda West. "Think Whole Foods meets In-N-Out Burgers," Amanda explains in defining her store's strategic design. I think Amanda's restaurant design is a role model for the industry's future.

America has approximately 200,000 fast food restaurants generating national annual revenues exceeding $120 billion (Hoovers). The classic success formula for a fast food restaurant is to conveniently offer competitively priced comfort food. This industry has grown from its 1950's hamburger/hotdog roots into a diversity of foods types and restaurant formulas. While the names of internationally branded companies like McDonalds, Burger King, Wendy's or KFC dominate our collective consciousness the industry is actually highly fragmented with the top 50 sized companies accounting for only 25% of sales.

And the entire restaurant industry is under tremendous stress during this recession. A PricewaterhouseCoopers survey found that restaurant insolvencies in the first quarter of 2009 were 33% higher than the last quarter of 2008.

In comparison, Amanda's opened its doors in July 2008 and has achieved year over year sales increases while three nearby restaurants have been forced to close.

Amanda's Secret Green Sauce is selling healthy convenience food at competitive prices. My first meal at Amanda's was a veggie burger and apple fries that cost $6. It was my first veggie burger and I was stunned at how good it tasted. The apple fries were actually a sliced raw apple diced to look like French fries and served with a honey-yogurt dipping sauce rather than sugar-rich ketchup. The meal looked like fast food, tasted great and was priced like what I would normally pay at Top Dog, my favorite hot dog place up the street from Amanda's.

Amanda's success is supported by market research conducted by M/A/R/C Research that asked fast food customers how important it is to them that fast-food restaurants participate in green initiatives. Almost half of those surveyed felt a fast food restaurant's participation in green initiatives was either very important or extremely important. Reflecting the leadership role Concerned Caregivers (our moms) are playing in the adoption of sustainability, over half the women surveyed held this position.

"Approachable" is a how Amanda defines her strategy for creating a healthy fast food restaurant. Her goal is to remove the price, taste and convenience barriers that may have limited healthy dining's appeal to the mass market. She is achieving this goal by offering:

- Prices that attract budget-driven buyers

- A menu that is tasty and healthy

- Fast, efficient service that you would expect at a fast food restaurant

- A "feel good" environment that is created by offering a communal table where neighbors can meet, a highly motivated staff that senses each meal they serve could be opening the discovery door of healthy eating to yet another customer and a restaurant design that uses such things as Low-VOC paints so mothers can be comfortable that their children will not be exposed to toxins.

Amanda is also a green-realist, "We can't afford to do all organic." To be price competitive and still offer healthy food she uses all-natural meats with no hormone or anti-biotic agents. She does use organic cheeses, apples and greens. Her best selling item is the classic cheese-burger. It consists of all natural meat and organic cheese. The basic burger is a 3 ounce portion. Additional patties can be added. "My goal is to get people who never would consider eating a veggie burger to migrate from eating our healthy burgers to trying a veggie burger. And this approach is working, I am seeing customers who have never eaten a veggie burger trying one here," Amanda explains.

And she is always seeking continuous improvement from her supply chain to increase the restaurant's sustainability at competitive prices. "We timed it right for opening Amanda's," she explains. "Everything we serve including the napkins and utensils is compostable. But in 2007 the supply chain wasn't in place to achieve this result. Now, the only reason we have a trash can is to collect what customers bring into our store that needs to be thrown away."

Amanda's is also a classic example of "Know it, Embrace" marketing that engages rather than advertises. To increase awareness and store traffic Amanda held an anniversary free-raffle for her customers that gave away gifts contributed by area merchants. The contributing merchants received marketing exposure to her customers. Customers signing up for the raffle included their emails that Amanda now uses for ongoing outreach. Gifts were raffled 4 times an hour. Customer feedback was overwhelmingly positive. At a time of economic recession one winning customer told Amanda, "Winning this gift gives me hope." And the cost to Amanda for creating this increased awareness and positive feelings among her customers? Nothing more than time.

Amanda has applied a similar strategy with her work associates or her "team" as she calls them. A key element in creating the team was in defining a mantra that would clearly articulate to associates what the company stood for and how it would make decisions. The mantra

Amanda chose was "Healthy Community." This phrase is something all of her associates related to. It was easy for them to remember and it represented what they wanted to be part of. When confronted with those "fork-in-the-road" decisions every business confronts the team asks themselves which fork is most supportive of achieving a "Healthy Community."

There are several challenges that Amanda's restaurant faces as a start-up company in a highly competitive market space. Her restaurant can't compete against the chain's 99 cents loss leader offerings. She is also still looking for that "sustainable toy" to compete against the toys being given away in the major chain's youth-promotions. And of course the advertising campaigns of the national brands are many times larger than Amanda's annual revenues. But what Amanda has created is a path toward winning market share in a $120 billion annual revenue industry by aligning with the Concerned Caregivers' and the Millennial Generation's search for ""cost less, mean more"" fast food that is healthy to eat, served in a toxin-free environment and operated in a sustainable manner.

Vision

Like Amanda's case study, all entrepreneurial enterprises (either as stand alone companies or business units within a larger corporation) begin with a vision. And the successful businesses are the ones that have visions focused upon the customer. **It is extremely important for green-entrepreneurs with a passion for enhancing sustainability to also have their passion focused upon what sells to the Awareness Customer**^{TM}. *The path for executing a* *green business vision runs through the hearts and desires of the Awareness Customer™.*

Strategy

Vision drives strategy design. The enabling elements of a successful green business strategy include these three ingredients of The Secret Green Sauce™:

1. Aligning Value with Values
2. Prove It, Conclusively
3. "Know it, Embrace it."

Aligning Value with Values is your pricing strategy for gaining at least price parity with the competing 20th Century solutions that your sustainable goods and services will replace. Why is price parity so important? **Market research indicates that if all things are equal, including price, The Awareness Customer™ will buy the green product or service rather than the unsustainable solution.** This is a huge revenue growth opportunity for a green business or a business seeking to grow revenues by going green. And especially in this recession it is a path for preserving revenues based upon market research that consumers are less likely to cut their expenditures they believe serve a greater good for themselves, their loved ones and their future.

Prove it, Conclusively! is your branding strategy. Credibility, credibility, credibility are the three goals for branding green goods and services. Consumers are confused on what is green and what businesses are green. The companies and products that are growing green revenues are doing a great job of helping the Awareness Customer™ answer their credibility questions by linking their products to highly credible third party alliances and endorsements. This is especially important based upon market research that indicates that green is a key element in an Awareness Customer's™ "impulse" or unplanned purchase actions. So this "linking" to credible third parties is an especially important element for your product labels.

"Know it, Embrace it" is your marketing plan. The Awareness Customer™ is accessed via Web 2.0. They are searching Web 2.0 for paths to implement their Sustainability 2.0 goals on research, education and implementation.

The first step in marketing to the Awareness Customer™ is a process of engagement that begins with *their* focus upon an issue or question.

The marketing action-path toward mass marketing progresses through these three steps:

1. *Awareness* of your value proposition

2. *Experimentation* that enables the Awareness Customer™ early-adopters to gain experience on you and your products, and most importantly, to gain their invaluable feedback

3. *Procurement* as the Awareness Customers™ literally "buys-in" to your green business solutions. Isn't this the story of Amanda's? She offers a natural meat cheeseburger with organic cheese and greens but her customers are moving toward experimenting, and then buying, the healthier items on the menu like a veggie burger.

Getting To First Base

How you get to first base with your Secret Green Sauce strategy is critical to building toward:
1. Price leadership
2. Stakeholder alliances
3. Enabling cash flow to fuel growth.

How to answer the question of "where is first base" is through identifying the customer's "burning platform." A burning platform is a strong, often passionate need, of a customer defined as something they will pay for right now, namely a fire extinguisher! Figure out how your business is a fire extinguisher to a customer's "burning platform" and you will have found your first base for building your business.

What Amanda did in designing Amanda's was attempt to remove the need to say "no" for a customer to buy healthy food. This is the "burning platform" for customers, how can you eat well, affordably and healthily? "Unlike ordering at Subway where you have to say no to things like mayonnaise and processed cheese you only have to say yes at my restaurant to order a healthy, tasty and affordable meal," Amanda explains.

And a foundational element in building your fire extinguisher is a Crossing the Pricing Chasm™ plan. It is absolutely critical you have such a plan and that you achieve this plan. "Paying more to go green" is, at best, a niche market strategy. But market research does say the Awareness Customer™ is very motivated to buy if your green solution "costs less and means more." Amanda's is not the cheapest fast food but it is affordable. The restaurant has achieved a "Crossing The Pricing Chasm™" result.

The Crossing the Pricing Chasm™ plan is a process for moving your business from a pricing beach head with early adopter Awareness Customers™ who will pay more to go green toward achieving at least pricing parity of not price leadership for your green solution compared to the current 20th Century "unsustainable" business system. Designing/implementing a Crossing the Pricing Chasm™ plan is a main barrier for too many start-up green-entrepreneurs. They have wonderful visions for making the world a better place to live in and they can experience initial success because their vision is so aligned with the vision held by early-adopter Awareness Customers™. But as they grow they hit the "price competitive wall" where the majority of consumers are not looking to pay more for green. A second variation is where they hit the pricing wall because competitors (often legacy 20th century companies looking to grow green revenues) emerge with lower prices. A major "getting to first base" goal is to build toward achieving a ""cost less, mean more"" solution that can be mass marketed to the Awareness Customer™ and sustained in the face of price competition threats.

And "first base" is also defined as a business successfully, and creditably, plugging into the Awareness Customer Dynamic™. This is hugely important in building credibility for your green product in your "Prove it, Conclusively!" branding effort. First base in branding follows the path of creating awareness within Web 2.0 of your competitively shaped green solution and gaining the Awareness Customer's™ feedback/testimonials. Many pioneering green-entrepreneurs that have been successful in building this type of brand equity were able to sell their green business at a handsome stock valuation based upon this brand equity and Awareness Customer™ loyalty to a larger company seeking a path for growing green revenues.

"Cash is king" is not a unique mantra for entrepreneurs. For many green-entrepreneurs who have their passions focused upon a vision of a better world I re-label this cliché as "Cash is Green" and list it as a major step in Getting To First Base out of recognition that the majority of start-up businesses fail due to a lack of capital. The Achilles heel of most entrepreneurs, including green ones, is that they over estimate the size and timing of revenues and underestimate costs. One consulting exercise I use in working with early-stage companies is to slash their revenue projections by half, cut their prices by 20% and double their costs. The typical result is a financial model that crashes. This sobering exercise works wonders in helping the management team to focus upon a "cash-survivalist" mentality that will sustain the business until the vision for revenues, prices and economies of scale on costs actually materialize (and I help the early-stage management team develop cash preservation strategies for achieving their early-stage performance milestones). And because Cash is Green is this important I have included it in the recipe for "The Secret Green Sauce™".

The early-stage lessons on cash preservation are especially important in selling green to customers who are price sensitive, who are confused on what is green and where the competitive landscape is populated by legacy 20th Century competitors who have the money, power and motivation to execute strategies for predatory actions to blunt the emergence of sustainable competitors. Being pure of heart is a commendable quality among many green-entrepreneurs but being a fierce, practical competitor capable of managing a business around cash flows is an imperative for building a successful business, including a green business. Successful green early-stage companies have strongly detailed cash preservation action-items for achieving their Getting To First Base milestones that recognize the reality that revenues almost never come in as large or as fast as planned and that there are typically unpleasant cost surprises that have tobe managed without crashing a company's path to first base.

"Cost less, Mean more"

After rounding first base your path toward home plate is defined by:

1. Gaining price-parity with the competing 20th Century unsustainable solutions

2. Growing market leading credibility with the Awareness Customer™.

You are now executing the next phase of Crossing The Green Pricing Chasm™ strategy, managing green growth. Your green revenues are growing as more Awareness Customers™ discover your business and products offer them less cost, more meaning. You have the positive cash flow to grow your green product line in progression with the Awareness Customer's™ procurement decision process of research, experimentation and then procurement. Your successful engagement in the Awareness Customer Dynamic™ is generating a growing number of customer endorsements that grow your brand equity which attracts more Awareness Customers™. And your participation in the Awareness Customer Dynamic™ is shaping your product designs. It is also driving your human resource talent pool as you hire associates aligned with the vision you are achieving. And most importantly, your eye is always focused upon building price leadership.

Managing growth is now your business challenge.

Like Amanda West, the founder of Amanda's healthy fast food restaurant, you are in green-entrepreneur heaven!

Chapter Nine

Terroir
Green-entrepreneurship

Terroir is a French word most familiarly applied to the wine growing appellations like Burgundy or Champagne or Napa. "Taste of earth" is an English translation that seems to embody the French essence of the word as applied to wine. The agriculture industry uses this word to capture how the combination of the soil, climate, exposition and tradition will influence a crop and the production of products like wine.

Al Courchesne, owner of Frog Hollow Farm, is the green-entrepreneur who introduced me to "Terroir" and its huge implications for green-entrepreneurship. Frog Hollow Farm organically grows fruit. Their fruit is so rich and delicious that it is served at Alice Water's Chez Panisse, an internationally acclaimed fountainhead of organic and locally grown dining. And his fruit is prominently displayed in Frog Hollow Farm branded cartons by Whole Foods. How much respect has Al's fruit generated? When he took his wife Becky to Chez Panisse for their anniversary the chefs invited them to sit at their private chef's table in the kitchen!

While Al is a great farmer he is also a role-model for green-entrepreneurship. He has succeeded in creating a modern business enterprise employing over 60 associates that produce organically grown fruit, pastries and various jams/jellies under the unifying brand of Frog Hollow Farm.

He also has created a multi-tiered sales channel strategy that includes:

- Restaurants

- Grocery stores

- His own retail store located in San Francisco's Ferry Building

- A Community Supported Agriculture (CSA) service that sells directly to consumers through monthly and annual subscriptions that offer regular delivery of seasonal foods

- Participation in San Francisco's Saturday farmers market.

I gained the following definition for Terroir from studying Frog Hollow farms and Al's entrepreneurship:

"Terrior is the sum effect green entrepreneurship has in defining products that meet the Awareness Customer's™ search for "cost less, mean more"."

The concept of "Terroir" appears to capture the essence of The Secret Green Sauce™ applied to green-entrepreneurship. Success as a green-enterprise is a **_sum effect_** of:

1. Environmental responsibility

2. A high level of creditability

3. Brand leveraging

4. Multi-channel sales outreach

5. Personal service

6. Ingenuity

7. Competitive pricing.

Here are the lessons learned from how Frog Hollow Farm has applied "Terroir":

Environmental Responsibility.

Success at selling green begins with environmental stewardship. This is the foundational core of being green but this singular trait or expertise is not enough to grow a green-business. Al is an expert at organic fruit farming that satisfies the Awareness Customers'™ search for organically grown and locally produced food. He continues to explore for ideas in his business to gain a "darker shade" of green. But, in terms of green-entrepreneurship his expertise as an organic farmer is but the foundation upon which he has applied his talents as an exceptionally astute businessman.

Creditability.

Creditability is hugely important. The Awareness Customer™ measures it at the product, human resources and corporate levels. Al is hugely credible from the moment you meet him in his bib-overalls and you shake his farmer-hard hand. His products "walk-the-talk" in terms of quality, taste and size. And Frog Hollow Farm as a corporation is ethical and customer oriented. They are the "whole package" that customers are looking for.

Branding.

Frog Hollow Farm has achieved brand identity and a loyal brand following. Al humbly gives Whole Foods credit for his branding success. Whole Foods believed in his product enough to display them in Frog Hollow Farm branded cartons at prominent locations within their store. This is a classic example of brand leveraging that is a credit both to Al and Whole Foods. Brand leveraging with an established brand leader is a very cost effective path for building brand equity for early-stage green entrepreneurs. And brand leveraging, step-by-step, is growing in influence as the Awareness Customer "connect the dots" on the brands they are experimenting with and then committing to.

Sales/Revenue Strategy.

Candidly, I was blown away by Al's sales channel plan. Like all successful entrepreneurs he understands his operating and profit margins by customer and product. And the direct sale of his branded product to the end-use consumer is his highest-margin sales channel. As Al explains, "A farmer selling a commodity to a middleman is a low margin business but a business selling a branded product to the consumer can earn attractive profit margins." Al's brand is clearly displayed on the menu at Chez Panisse, in Whole Foods and through his direct retail sales channels. In the business of selling fruit that some business people would view as a commodity product Al has created higher margins by selling a branded product in a highly sophisticated multi-tier sales channel strategy. This same opportunity is there to be harvested by green-entrepreneurs across the range of green goods and services as consumers shift their procurement loyalties toward sustainability.

And the other advantage of a multi-tier sales channel strategy is revenue flow. You can imagine the annual revenue curve for selling fruit as being shaped like a steep mountain, namely a large percentage of revenues accrued during a relatively short harvesting time period. Al's multi-channel sales approach, especially the CSA sales channel, affords the ability to fill in the troughs of lower revenue time periods. This is ever so important as bank loans and other sources of working capital are impacted by the recession and our emergence from a historical credit crisis event.

Personal Service.

All of us who have experienced the frustration of an automated answering system that now is the standard operating procedure offered by much of Corporate America can appreciate the value of personal service. I raise as an interesting question whether including personal service should be included in a definition of sustainability? I know it is a competitive advantage in business compared to the current growing alternative of wasting time punching numbers in answer to computer generated questions only to be connected too often to a customer service representative unable to satisfy the customer inquiry either due to a lack of empowerment or product knowledge. If you call or visit Frog Hollow Farm you will talk to real people who are very knowledgeable about their product and their ability to meet performance targets on price and timing. Personal service is what I am seeing as an emerging competitive advantage offered by green-entrepreneurs. It saves times, it is efficient and therefore fits my definition of sustainability.

Ingenuity.

Ingenuity is a common trait among the successful green-entrepreneurs in my network. Six Sigma and other corporate improvement processes are hugely valuable tools. But too often I have also seen these valuable tools applied by committees in a manner that created motion/measurement/reports but not necessarily meaningful results. What was missing was the power of imagination <u>enabled by an entrepreneurial-risk-spirit that appreciates there is high value in trying and failing</u> as part of a process of creating sustained competitive advantages through ongoing "outside the box" questioning, learning and product/organizational development. Al has a long list of ideas he is pursuing to cut costs, develop new products, increase brand equity and find new customers. He allocates a portion of his company's time and money in pursuit of ingenious solutions. He is disciplined in his analysis but it is his entrepreneurial appetite for risk taking, not an analytical process, which drives his creative search for business improvement. The green businesses, or green business units within Corporate America, that I see as being successful have a green-entrepreneur in a leadership role with the power to take the risk of failing in pursuit of ingenuity.

Competitive Pricing.

I had the opportunity to overhear Al handing numerous phone calls from commercial customers seeking a supplier-bid. Price and delivery schedule were always key elements of these conversations. Al grows great tasting fruit in an environmentally sustainable manner but ultimately his prices have to be competitive for him to close a sale. Customers want to buy products with more meaning if they are price competitive.

Green-Entpreneurship

Based upon my observation of green-entrepreneurs the concept of "Terroir" is emerging into a mega-trend within the Green Economic Revolution. The concept's application captures these *sum-effects* of green entrepreneurship:

- Much of our current green-entrepreneurship is typically local or regional in its inspiration but collectively they are merging into global solutions.

- Most green entrepreneurs are specialists at a trade or science who, through trial and error, are gaining market traction with customers seeking businesses and products that satisfying specific environmental or wellness expectations.

- The personal touch of human service is attractively provided by these green-entrepreneurs in a manner that plugs into the "learning, experimentation, procurement" process used by the early-adopter Awareness Customer.

- These bottom-line motivated entrepreneurs are pioneering how to offer sustainability and wellness solutions at competitive prices.

- Their entrepreneurship is not shaped by policy directives or management process tools but rather by individual ingenuity including the willingness to take experimental risks in a continuous search for competitive advantage based a foundational goal for achieving sustainable results.

Like a wine appellation, green-entrepreneurship at this dawning of the Green Economic Revolution is offering distinctive, local, personalized sustainability/wellness-solutions at competitive prices influenced by their own "Terroir".

"The Secret Green Sauce"

Chapter Ten

Green Business Development
Growing Green Entrepreneurs

971 mayors have joined The U.S. Conference of Mayors' Climate Protection Agreement and its commitment to reduce carbon emissions in their cities below 1990 levels, in line with the Kyoto Protocol. Cities across America are taking the initiative to promote green-entrepreneurship for the following reasons:

1. Local jobs. Green industries solve local problems with local work associates.

2. Tax Revenues. Local green businesses pay local taxes.

3. Citizen Benefits. From lower electric bills, to less traffic congestion, to clear air, the politics for going green are most evident when successfully implemented at the local level.

Here are examples of cities and there pioneering green companies that are creating green-jobs, a stronger local economy and a cleaner environment:

Austin, Texas is where I begin this list because I like people who take on ambitious goals. And Austin has established an Austin Climate Protection Program with the goal of making Austin "...the leading city in the nation in the fight against climate change." Toward achieving this goal their municipal utility is building a 30 MW solar power plant. The City has established a "zero waste" goal that aligns with the U.N. Urban Environmental Accord's goal to reduce the per capita solid waste disposal to landfills by 20% by 2012 and achieve zero waste by 2040.

San Jose, California has bold plans for being the electric car capital of the world. San Jose is located minutes from Sand Hill Road, a non-descript cluster of two story office buildings that house some of the world's leading venture capital firms that have financed such companies as Hewlett Packard and Google. The city has used its proximity to this heartland of technology innovation to land Telsa motors, a pioneering electric car company. Telsa and the city have announced a $250 million factory. And why did Telsa locate in San Jose? According to Zee'ev Drori, Chief Technology Office for Telsa, "The heart and soul of the electric car is the electric drive train, and for that, we need the types of skills located here." The city estimates the regional economic impact from the Telsa factory to be $2 billion a year.

SustainLane has bestowed upon *Portland, Oregon* the title of greenest city in America. SustainLane bases its city ranking upon the criteria of healthy air and drinking water and the availability of parks and public transit systems. It also considers the sustainability of the local economy in terms of green buildings, farmer markets and use of renewable energy and alterative fuels. The green expertise of Portland's architects and building companies is gaining national and global demand. An Australian building contracting company named Cardno, Ltd acquired Portland-based WRG Design Inc. for the stated reason of acquiring WRG's intellectual capital on green building practices. Green Building Services, Inc. is a company that began as a business unit of Portland Electric that spun off to create a leading energy efficiency company with six staff members now serving on the U.S. Building Council that created the LEED certification process.

Boston, Massachusetts area is home to Enernoc, one of the first green companies to successfully have an Initial Public Offering. Enernoc's product is a demand response system that enables customers to harvest lower electric bills by either removing electrical load or self-generating electricity during a utility's highest priced time periods. And it is also home to A123, a pioneering lithium ion battery company that Chevrolet has announced will supply the batteries for the electric car Volt. And Boston is home to Evergreen, a solar panel company which recently broke ground on a 100 MW manufacturing plant in Wuhan, China.

And a pioneering example of Green Economic Development is *Palm Desert, California.* This is a community built upon vacation and retirement homes attracted to the desert's warm climate and clean air. It is also a community whose elected officials are all Republican. But as Councilman Jim Ferguson, City of Palm Desert (R), explains, going green "...is not a partisan issue, it is a common sense issue." And the green common sense as applied by the City of Palm Desert is to help their citizens lower their energy bills while preserving the pristine environment that this community so loves. The City has set a goal of reducing electricity consumption by 30%. Let me be clear, this is not reducing the electricity consumption at city buildings. This goal is for reducing the community of Palm Desert's electricity consumption. To achieve this goal the City is offering loans to its homeowners and businesses to install more efficient air conditioning units and roof top solar systems. The loans are paid back through property taxes paid by the home or building owner. The typical result is the building uses about 40% less electricity and achieves about a 50% reduction in electric bills. Applied to the City's targeted 22,000 dwelling units this program will pump approximately $45 million into their local economy.

One of the companies that was started to fulfill this green business opportunity is called Renova Energy Corp. This company offers home owners a free audit to identify and rank by least cost/highest payback the actions a homeowner can take to lower their electric bills through conservation and installation of solar panels. Renova offers a broad range of technologies from solar attic fans, to tinted windows to roof top solar systems. The typical homeowner begins their process of greening their homes by installing lower cost items that on average reduce their energy consumption by about 25%.

And Renova' President, Vince Bataglia, is the type of visionary entrepreneur who sees that a business is more than just making a profit. He helped to set up a Green Zone Campus to train people on the green jobs that are emerging in his community. And this Green Zone Campus serves as an incubation location for start up green companies. The Campus is aligned with the local university to offer courses on entrepreneurship and the Palm Desert community's efforts at creating sustainable economic development, job training and entrepreneurship that holds the potential of turning the desert "green."

Paul Hietter is Executive Chef and President of Love At First Bite Catering & Event Planning serving the Palm Desert and Palm Springs area. He is finding that his customers are now adopting going green beyond the focus upon energy. They are asking about organic foods and in response Paul is an active buyer at the local farmers market. He recently catered the wedding of Leslie Shilcott, a producer of Al Gore's internationally acclaimed documentary An Inconvenient Truth. As you would expect the entire event was designed to be sustainable down to the use of soy candles, the serving of organic beverages and use of pitcher-water rather than bottled water. And Paul caters the film crews from Hollywood that shoot in the area's picturesque scenery. This key customer requires that nothing be left behind and that the shooting site is as pristine as when they first arrived. And most encouraging, Paul is seeing that his customers are increasingly focused upon what is served to their children. Of course, wellness is a major sustainability trend for Concerned Caregivers and a business opportunity for green-entrepreneurs like Paul.

A very interesting book that aligns with what I am seeing in my green business network is "The Small-Mart Revolution" by Michael Shuman which outlines a vision where "local businesses are beating the global competition." In concert this aligns with my observation that the local American enterprise is again the engine of innovation, this time it is green-innovation. And they are often being supported by their city-elected officials who see in green-entrepreneurship the jobs, services and environmental benefits their electorate is seeking.

The lessons learned from cities like Austin, Portland and Palm Desert in growing green businesses, green jobs and green-tax revenues are:

1. Prime the Financial Pump.
    Going green needs capital because going green is often what economists call a "substitution effect" where a customer buys a capital goods item like a roof top solar power system rather than an "operating cost" like buying monthly electricity from a utility. By enabling the financing of capital goods a government achieves a "pay-back" through economic development that creates local jobs, a higher quality of life for the community, increased local tax revenues and of course, earnings on the financing.

2. Build Local.
Being local is a competitive advantage in going green. It is community agriculture vs. industrial agriculture. It is recycling existing building to a higher and better use vs. building new towns out of former agricultural land. It is domestic innovation vs. global mass production that emits global mass pollution. It is hundreds of small green-entrepreneurs focused upon delivering the individual attention the Awareness Customer™ needs to enable their process of learning, experimentation and then green procurement.

3. Green Incubation.
The implementation of green is not exclusively "small." Green, like any other industry, will mature to achieve economies of scale that enables winning pricing parity compared to the 20th Century legacy systems that are increasingly costing more, delivering less. There will be "Telsa Motors" or "First Solar" scale manufacturing that will provide large numbers of highly attractive green jobs. And the path for gaining these hugely attractive economic development opportunities is to nurture these opportunities during their incubation stage. Communities that are slow to search for and nurture their green-entrepreneurs will be at a competitive disadvantage in realizing the opportunity of green economic development. One of the ideas I like in The Small-Mart Revolution is the concept of "identify leaks." This is an audit process a community should do to identify where they now rely upon imports for goods and services that could, alternatively, be produced locally by their own green-entrepreneurs.

In summary, while Federal policy is often caught up in the creation of 1400+ pages of legislation like that in the Waxman-Markey Climate Bill the spirit of entrepreneurship is on fire at the local level in cities across America. Small green companies are growing into larger ones that are creating new jobs and increased local tax revenues. And helping to stimulate and enable this green entrepreneurship are cities like Palm Desert that are using political leadership and financial innovation to create a cleaner local environment and increased prosperity.

"The Secret Green Sauce"

Chapter Eleven

Resources
"Where To Begin"

Successful businesses have as their foundation a strong understanding of their customers' needs. The best ones are "inside" their customer's minds and, most especially, their hearts. The following are resources to help you begin this process that I have organized by the topic of:

- Associations/Non-profits
  These associations and non-profits provide insights on green jobs and green business opportunities.

- Awareness Customer
  Market research and insights on the Awareness Customer.

- Business
  Resources for green business managers and green-entrepreneurs.

- Stockholder Valuation
  Insights on how going green is increasing stockholder valuations.

Awareness Customer

BuyGreen.com: http://www.buygreen.com/ This site deploys a methodology for evaluating what is "green" that I reference to evaluate green products. These folks are pretty attuned to the Concerned Caregiver market segment of Awareness Customers™. If you are designing a green product I would calibrate your design against their methodology to get a feel how your target market might evaluate your product in terms of "Prove It, Conclusively!

Good Guide: http://www.goodguide.com/ is a highly credible site that reviews products and their supplying companies. This is a great place for green-businesses to gain an understanding on the issues that can impact the perceptions of the Awareness Customer™.

Treehugger.com and Planet Green:
http://www.treehugger.com/
I have more than a few good friends who would rather eat tofu than click on Treehugger.com. That is their loss. This is one of my favorite sites for learning about what the Awareness Customer is thinking and who is doing what. And their sister site at Planet Green has a section "How to go green" that covers just about every topic you can image.

http://planetgreen.discovery.com/go-green/green-index/green-index.html

Associations/Non-profits

Dream Green Jobs:
http://www.sustainablebusiness.com/index.cfm
/go/greendreamjobs.main/?CFID=12859499&CF
TOKEN=46921511 has job posting for jobs with a
focus upon work with government agencies and non-
profits:

Green   Restaurant   Association:
http://www.dinegreen.com/ is a pioneering
organization that is really making a difference in
greening our restaurant industry. They have been
working in the "trenches" since the 1990's and are now
experiencing explosive growth as restaurants large and
small realize that sustainability creates profits, sales and
customer loyalty. A must visit site if you own a
restaurant!

Eco-libris: There mission is to making going green easy
and affordable. I pay them to plant a tree in an
economically disadvantaged country for every book I
sell. Their site reviews books and ideas on how to go
green: http://www.ecolibris.net/

Rainforest Alliance:
http://www.rainforest-alliance.org/ are the folks
we are really making a difference in helping companies
like Nestle and Caribou coffee sell products that
represent a high degree of ethics in terms of respect for
people and the environment. I look to them as a compass
on issues of "Prove It, Conclusively!"

Vote Solar: http://www.votesolar.org/ This the
advocacy group that helped create California's Million
Solar Home Program and who are working across the
country to shape regulation and legislation to allow roof
top solar systems connect to the utility system so that

solar energy can reduce a host site's electric bill or sell its electricity into the grid.

Business/Green-Entrepreneurship

Earth 2017:
http://www.earth2017.com is a site that blogs on best practices for building sustainable strategies for growing green revenues. It is also the website of this book's author.

Green Drinks:
http://www.greendrinks.org/ is my idea of networking, meeting people who share my passion for building green businesses and happy hour! They have events across the country and around the world. Also a good event if you are networking as part of a career transition.

Green Architecture and Building Report:
http://www.gabreport.com is a fantastic information warehouse on green trends and innovations in green building.

New Voice of Business:
http://www.newvoiceofbusiness.org/ is a model for a "new" chamber of commerce that informs, engages, and mobilizes a business people. Elliot Hoffman, a restaurateur who created the business called "Just Desserts" founded New Voice of Business and he has assembled an impressive array of board members and advisors that are representative of green-entrepreneurship.

Renova Energy Corp.:
http://renova360.com/index.html is a green business in Palm Desert, California that is a good example for smaller green-businesses on how to "do it right." They have a get to first base pricing strategy of

first reducing a home's or business' energy consumption and then selling them a solar power system that is sized to this reduced demand for energy. And they are creating jobs and helping to train the future green work force through involvement in the City's Green Zone Campus.

Sustainable Business Alliance:
http://www.sustainablebiz.org/ is located in Berkeley and from this location they intersect with some of the cutting edge business innovators in green entrepreneurships. Mark McLeod their Executive Director is a thought-leader for businesses and communities looking to go green.

Sustainable Silicon Valley:
www.sustainablesiliconvalley.org is a website with some great ideas for how to build and implement green teams.

Walmart: If you need proof that sustainability is a business opportunity then please visit:
http://walmartstores.com/Sustainability/8844.aspx.
which links to their Sustainability 2.0 video. Watch and realize that sustainability is not something that is going to happen in the future. A Green Economic Revolution has begun and a global retailer is re-engineering their business model to realize this opportunity.

Glossary of Terms

Aligning Value with Values. A best practice used by successful green businesses and green-entrepreneurs in developing their pricing strategy. They begin with a price competitive focus for offering a green solution rather than a first focus upon solving an environmental problem.

Awareness Customer™. Three major consumer groups are driving the Green Economic Revolution. They are:
1. Concerned Caregivers
2. CEOs
3. Millennials.

Awareness Customer Dynamic™. The process for Know it, Embrace it" that is the interaction of learning/sharing via Web 2.0 and implementation via Sustainability 2.0. This is how many Awareness Customers (most especially Concerned Caregivers and Millennials) learn and it is the process through which they make informed decisions. This is the path for engaging the Awareness Customer.

Carbon-footprint Economic Analysis. A carbon footprint is a calculation of a company's emissions that typically includes the company' supply chain. The carbon-footprint economic analysis is an emerging calculation of growing business importance as governments require companies to report their economic risks tied to their environmental policies and carbon emissions.

CEOs. Increasing numbers of CEOs believe Global Warming is real, and man-made and their companies should reduce their carbon footprints to advert an environmental crisis. Over half of the Fortune 500 companies have established percentage goal for reducing their CO_2 emissions.

Collapse of "Unsustainability." The combination of upward price increases of 20th Century solutions and their increasing environmental/societal costs that are making these 20th Century goods and services less competitive compared to the growing number of sustainable solution alternatives.

Concerned Caregivers. It's our Moms! Concerned Caregivers are searching for sustainable solutions they often call "wellness" that will enhance the well-being of their loved ones.

""cost less, mean more"." The mantra of the Awareness Customer seeking to buy green. It is the business focus of successful green businesses.

"Cost More, Delivers Less." The growing awareness among customers that 20th Century solutions are charging them higher prices and negatively impacting the environment.

Crossing the Pricing Chasm™. A strategy for achieving the competitive positioning of ""cost less, mean more"." The first step is defining the price point that conveys price leadership. This is done through "aligning value with values." The process is one of achieving a beach head pricing position with early adopter customers and building from this beach head toward mass marketing price leadership.

Earth 2017™. An economic projection of a "tipping-point" projected to occur around 2017 when the goods and services of the Green Economic Revolution achieve price-parity with 20th Century goods and services. Achieving this pricing parity will stimulate $10 trillion in global annual revenue for sustainable goods and services.

Economies of Scale. The achievement of a downward price curve through mass production and learning that is achieved through moving forward on a learning curve for lowering per unit manufacturing costs. Sustainability is now moving into its Economies of Scale with the potential for green businesses to continuously offer lower prices for green goods and services.

Externalities. These are the "outside the box" impacts upon an economy or business that typically are not captured in a price established in a market place between buyers and sells focused upon a singular transaction (pollution, traffic congestion and "boots on the ground" protecting foreign oil fields are examples). The classic economic example of externalities is the story called A Tragedy of the Commons. It draws upon the time period in New England where towns had central commons that offered

Green Economic Revolution. A global shift in business systems toward a sustainable model that offers a less cost, more meaning alternative to 20th Century business systems that are increasingly costing more and delivering less.

Green Teams. A group organized to explore how their company can go green. Typical green teams are focused upon lowering costs, emissions and waste. Many green team are achieving demonstrable success and have become a significant implementation path for going green by Corporate America.

Greenwashing. Claims by companies and products for being environmentally responsible that are not true or have shades of gray within their claims. This is a HUGE issues for The Secret Green Sauce™ ingredient of Prove

It, Conclusively! It is also not a black and white issue. Visit http://www.goodguide.com and review their product ranking of Green Works. The product gets a respectable "green" ranking but Clorox the manufacturer receives a "brown" ranking. So is it greenwashing to represent Green Works as green?

HIP. The term and financial analysis methodology of R. Paul Herman of HIP Investor, Inc. which stands for: Human Impact + Profits.

Locavore. A person who eats locally produced and prepared food. New Oxford Dictionary selected Locavore as its word of the year.

Millennial Generation. The children of the boomer generation that almost matches the boomer generation in size and anticipated economic impacts as they enter their prime earning period. Millennials see sustainability as their future and place such a high level of importance upon buying sustainable goods and services that they are willing to pay more for these solutions.

Prove It, Conclusively! Due to green washing the path for gaining credibility with the Awareness Customers requires convincing documentation on the product's green benefits and the company's credibility often best demonstrated to the Awareness Customer through strategic allies.

Sustainability 2.0. The Awareness Customer's™ path for implementing their sustainability goals through the steps of
1. Research
2. Education
3. Application.

Check out Walmart's video entitled "Sustainability 2.0" on their website for an example of how this mega-company is pioneering going green.

Systems Thinking. Strategy tools for surfacing and quantifying the impacts of "externalities" (like a carbon tax on emissions or a shift in consumer buying behavior toward sustainability) upon a business. This inclusive process engages all stakeholders to surface their mental-models on how externalities will impact their decisions related to the company's business systems. One key tool is a "curve of change" (rarely is change linear, it is a most often a curve of initially-slower change that can accelerate as technologies, competitors and new customers emerge) that is an accumulation of potential change scenarios over time that are causal-loop algorisms calculated from stakeholder inputs. The value of this process is that it enables an enterprise-scale, "outside the silo," brainstorming utilizing a disciplined methodology grounded upon facts and knowledge harvested from structured interviews with customers, potential customers, regulators, opinion leaders, elected-officials, environmental-activists, competitors, work associates and management.

About the Author

Bill Roth is Entrepreneur.com's Green Business Coach and Founder of Earth 2017, a San Francisco-based firm helping companies grow green businesses.

He has also created the Green Entrepreneur Masters Certification Program.

Bill has been a pioneer in sustainability including participation in such marquee accomplishments as launching the first hydrogen-fueled Prius as a proof of concept, developing solar power systems using emerging technologies and the design of Real Time Pricing that has enabled consumer-acceptance of conservation technologies.

His public service has included being a corporate sponsor of California's pioneering legislation capping greenhouse gas emissions, serving on California's Hydrogen Highway Task Force and being a board member on his local community's sustainability group, Sustainable Moraga.

Bill is a professional economist with a Masters Degree in Economics from the University of Florida, has lectured in behalf of the World Bank, been published in professional economic and business journals and has submitted expert testimony on public policy issues.

www.ingramcontent.com/pod-product-compliance
Lightning Source LLC
Chambersburg PA
CBHW071909200326
41519CB00016B/4540